part of the parishfinder series

Published by ASPYE.
aspye@talktalk.net

A photographic and historical guide to the

Parish Churches
of
West Suffolk

compiled and photographed
by
Adrian S. Pye

Historical Notes

The parishes of West Suffolk are as defined by the Archdeaconry of Sudbury 1836. Included here are the parishes of Hadleigh, Monks Eleigh and Moulton, which were peculiars of Bocking in Essex, and of the Archbishop of Canterbury. Freckenham, which was a peculiar of the Bishop of Rochester in 1836, is also included. The deaneries of Hartismere and Stow, together with the parishes of Rickinghall Inferior, Rickinghall Superior and Hinderclay, were transferred to the Archdeaconry of Suffolk in 1837. All parishes are now in the diocese of St Edmundsbury and Ipswich.

Preface

It is through being involved in family history that I started photographing the churches where my family, at one time or another, had lived. More recently I have taken an interest in the architecture and development of the parish church. I started gathering together a collection of local churches for my own interest and I eventually decided to photograph every church in Suffolk a task that spanned three years. During my journeys through the county, I have seen some very interesting churches and have met some wonderfully interesting people. It is to these un-named people that I owe my thanks for their encouragement and assistance in compiling both publications.

Every church has been photographed from the outside, however difficult this was at times. It is because of the difficulty in some cases of capturing the whole church that I decided to make a contemporary record, hopefully before they were all surrounded by housing developments or had community centres and crèches built on the side of them. It is with regret that I did not start this endeavour 40 years ago, before the pressure of urban development took its toll. In truth, it is only since the development of the digital camera that I have been able to afford to take tens of thousands of photographs simply for the cost of a camera and a computer.

I would like to thank all the churches that were open to visitors and church crawlers such as myself and only wish there had been more. These days it is a risk to leave a church unlocked, but the risk has always been there. Look at the size of some of the iron-bound, triple-locked parish chests! Today's vandalism is nothing in comparison with the damage caused by the Puritans in the 16th century. It is arguable that an open church attracts visitors and therefore vandals are without opportunity. Unfortunately, some churches receive only one or two visitors each week. However, it has been said that 'a locked church is a dying church' and I do tend to agree. By discouraging visitors and expecting them to find a house a half a mile away in the hope that the key-holder is at home, or call a telephone number without the STD code, is a serious loss of potential revenue and support. It also causes frustration, especially if a notice proclaims 'Welcome to our Church'. A locked church is no good to man nor God. How much nicer it is, on turning the handle, the door creaks opens, and the mustiness of the fabric smacks you in the face.

Every church in the book was visited and photographed by me personally in an attempt to update the earlier writings and observations of others; but we are all fallible and I apologise in advance for any errors that may have crept into the text.

This is only intended as an easy to read guide to the parish church and is in no respect a complete reference. It is intended to be read by those who wish to pick out a church or churches they wish to visit, whether for family history research or simple curiosity.

I have found many delights in many churches, some that took my breath away in pure admiration. I found many disappointments too, and occasionally my heart sank when I saw the work of so-called restorers who had caused more damage than a shed-full of vandals.

Having completed East Suffolk in 2008 and warmly encouraged by sales and feedback from the readers, I ventured into West Suffolk. Now, with West Suffolk completed, I have decided to continue my mission into Norfolk. I have already found that it too has some outstanding churches to offer the church crawler. As with Suffolk, some are easier to photograph in their entirety than others, but every one is one step nearer to my goal of over 1300 churches in both counties.

Only the briefest of details have been included with each church and as previously mentioned, this is just a taste of what each one offers to the stranger and parishioner alike. The brevity of the notes does not necessarily indicate that the parish has little to offer the enquirer; it is simply a matter of how much one can fit onto a page.

Because of my interest in family history, the area covered is based on the Deaneries within the Archdeaconries of Sudbury and Suffolk as they were in 1836. All Suffolk parishes are now in the St. Edmundsbury and Ipswich Diocese unless stated to the contrary. The deaneries have changed too and are listed under 'Deanery 2000'.

Some Victorian and later churches have not been included as they are not the principal church of the parish. There are blank pages at the end of the book if you wish to include your choice or make personal notes.

The parishes are listed in alphabetical order and where a cardinal point precedes the name, it is treated as part of the name. e.g. West Stow, not Stow, (West). Some parishes are prefixed with Little or Great, others with Parva or Magna as a suffix. The listing in these cases, depends on common usage.

The Ordnance Survey grid references are for the parish church, the village centre is sometimes a considerable distance away. Postcodes are also given where available but these do not always relate precisely to the church itself, but sometimes relate to a house nearby.

A few parishes I have marked thus *****. These I commend to the reader as, in my own unqualified opinion, they are especially interesting historically and architecturally and always open or accessible during the day, or at least were at the time of writing. I have also marked some ****. These are also commended for reasons other than those with five stars.

I hope the reader enjoys reading this as much as I enjoyed gathering the contents and if in some small way I have encouraged others to visit our ecclesiastical heritage I consider my continuing labours worthwhile.

Adrian S. Pye.
Lowestoft, Suffolk. 2009

Table of Contents

The author gratefully acknowledges information obtained from the following sources:
White's Directory for Suffolk 1845 (Arthur White)
Suffolk Churches and Their Treasures (H. Munro Cautley)
The King's England, Suffolk (Arthur Mee)
Guide booklets supplied in the individual churches.
Ordnance Survey for the grid references and
Ipswich & Bury St Edmunds Diocese for the post codes and modern deaneries.

While every effort has been made to ensure accuracy; for any errors in this publication, I apologise. No liability can be accepted for any loss or damage caused by whatever means as a result of reading or following the directions given in this publication.

Published by ASPYE.
aspye@talktalk.net

Printed by Micropress Printers Halesworth

ISBN 978-0-9558797-1-5

ACTON

Dedication:	All Saints
No of Bells:	5
Deanery 1836:	Sudbury
Hundred:	Babergh
Union house:	Sudbury
Deanery 2000:	Sudbury

3 miles NE of Sudbury
between Long Melford &
Great Waldingfield. Lane off
the High Street, 100 yards
west of The Crown PH.
O.S. grid ref: TL 892452
Post Code: CO10 0BA

Known earlier as Aketon this parish is famous for its history, having
been owned by Robert de Buers in the reign of Edward I, and later
awarded to Henry, Lord Bouchier by Henry IV. The church and
tower (which is heavily buttressed against collapse) is beautifully
proportioned. The tower itself, rebuilt in 1923 is square and
embattled as is the 15th c. south aisle and the porch. Inside, there is a
carved set of Hanoverian Arms; and a brass to the aforementioned
Robert de Bures dated 1302, and others of interest. Between the north
aisle and the sanctuary is a canopied and pinnacled altar. A beautiful
and very finely carved white marble monument is to Robert Jennens
(1761) and his wife. This church has pterodactyls instead of bats!

1

ALDHAM

Dedication:	St Mary
No of Bells:	1
Deanery 1836:	Sudbury
Hundred:	Cosford
Union house:	Semer
Deanery 2000:	Hadleigh

1½ miles NE of Hadleigh between Hadleigh & Elmsett. Almost a mile south-west of Aldham village near Aldham Hall. O.S. grid ref: TM 040444 Post Code: IP7 6NP

The church was built around 1350 but has been heavily restored, as has the round tower with its small spire surmounting it. There is an absence of dressed quoin stones which are substituted by bits of ancient coffin lids and boulders. The visitor will find, built into the jamb of a window south of the nave, fragments of a cross that is believed to be late Saxon. The piscina is 13th c. with engaged shafts and a moulded arch. One of the many ancient oak pews bears the date 1537. The font is a curious square shape with a central shaft and a column at each corner. The lectern is beautifully carved and has its original mediaeval base. The Royal Arms of George III hang above the 16th c. tower arch. Some of the woodwork is modern.

ALPHETON

Dedication:	Sts Peter & Paul	
No of Bells:	2	
Deanery 1836:	Sudbury	
Hundred:	Babergh	
Union house:	Sudbury	
Deanery 2000:	Sudbury	

6 miles N of Sudbury
between Bradfield Combust &
Long Melford. Off the Bury
Road (A134) at the southern-
most end of Church Lane.
O.S. grid ref: TL 873504
Post Code: CO10 9BJ

Over a half-mile from the village centre, next to the old Alpheton Hall, this fine church was snatched from ruins only last century. There is a fine 15th c. south doorway carved with pomegranates and roses in the porch, alongside a decorated holy water stoup. The 15th c. porch is made from oak but over time has been considerably repaired. The purbeck marble base of the present octagonal font is that of a much earlier example. The crudely painted Arms of Charles II hang in the nave inscribed "God Save the King". The 14th c. piscina and sedilia still retain part of the fine pinnacled & crocketted ogee arches. Poor box pews fill the nave and one stall with carved arm rests has the remains of mutilated misericordes.

AMPTON

Dedication:	St Peter
No of Bells:	4
Deanery 1836:	Thedwastre
Hundred:	Thedwastre
Union house:	Bury St Edmunds
Deanery 2000:	Ixworth

5 miles N of Bury St Edmunds between Ingham & Livermere: turn east off the A134 at Ingham then north into the main street. O.S. grid ref: TL 866712
Post Code: IP31 1NX

This little church has many curiosities to interest the visitor. There is a stoup just inside the south door. In the north of the nave is a chantry chapel, inscribed above "CAPELLA PERPETUE CANTARIE - JOH'IS COKET". The right to this perpetual chantry was granted in 1479. The Royal Arms are carved from wood and are believed to be those of Charles I. In the vestry are the Hanoverian Arms, unusually, painted on copper. The real treasure of the church is its 'Sealed Book' which is very rare, with a complicated history, and can only be viewed on request. Admiral Fitzroy was born in Ampton in 1805. He initiated weather forecasting and the maintaining of records in 1861. The monument to James Calthorpe (1536) is massive, and worth seeing.

ASPALL

Dedication:	St Mary of Grace	
No of Bells:	1	
Deanery 1836:	Hartismere	
Hundred:	Hartismere	
Union house:	Eye & Wortham	
Deanery 2000:	Loes	

6 miles S of Eye, between Thorndon & Debenham: take Little London Hill north from Debenham, for 1 mile. (Between cottages). O.S. grid ref: TM 167649
Post Code: IP14 6NY

There is a wooden north porch and a scratch dial on the south nave buttress. The font is a traditional East Anglian type. The Holy table is of Stuart date. The 13th c. church itself holds very little of interest to the historian although some of the animal carvings on the bench ends are worth viewing.   Anne Francis Chevallier daughter of John, famous as an agriculturalist, was born here in 1845 and was later to marry Henry Kitchener and become the mother of the future Lord Kitchener. There is a memorial to him in the church. Aspall Hall is far more interesting than the church: for centuries it has been the seat of the renowned Suffolk Chevallier family who gave their name to Chevallier Street in Ipswich.

ASSINGTON		4 miles SE of Sudbury
Dedication:	St Edmund	between Leavenheath &
No of Bells:	4	Newton. Turn south off
Deanery 1836:	Sudbury	A134 into Assington Park,
Hundred:	Babergh	by Assington Hall.
Union house:	Sudbury	O.S. grid ref: TL 935388
Deanery 2000:	Sudbury	Post Code: CO10 5LQ

Assington church was built by Canute the Great on the site of the last battle between the Saxons and the Danes. The Danes were victorious and built a church to give thanks. It has since been very heavily restored and virtually rebuilt. The western square tower has turret stairs which continue above the attractively embattled parapet. The 15th c. porch has stone benches and engaged vaulting shafts in the roof. A south aisle was added at a later date and contains many monuments to the Gurdon family. The wall mounted memorial for Brampton Gurdon (1648) and his two wives Elizabeth and Meriall is particularly attractive. The war memorial in the churchyard is of an unusually intricate design and it too bears the Gurdon name.

BACTON

Dedication:	St Mary
No of Bells:	6
Deanery 1836:	Hartismere
Hundred:	Hartismere
Union house:	Eye & Wortham
Deanery 2000:	Stowmarket

5 miles N of Stowmarket between Wyverstone & Cotton. Turn off the B1113 under railway bridge & follow to Church Road.
O.S. grid ref: TM 053672
Post Code: IP14 4LL

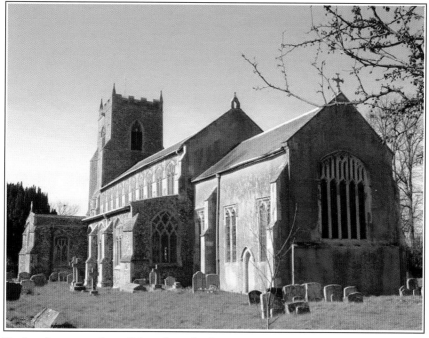

Early photographs of the church show a square tower with a fine 18th c. slate-covered spire, increasing the height by half as much again; but it became unsafe and was removed in 1935. At the apex of the nave the sanctus bellcote remains, although the bell has long gone. The nave has a clerestory with ten fine windows on each side and a splendid double hammerbeam roof. Over the chancel arch the remains of a doom can be seen with the dead rising from their graves. Parts of the rood and parclose screen remain but much was destroyed during restoration in 1864. There are a couple of benches with finely traceried ends with buttressed arm rests and grotesques. The 16th c. font has one plain face suggesting it once stood against a wall or pier.

BADWELL ASH

Dedication:	St Mary	
No of Bells:	5	
Deanery 1836:	Blackbourn	
Hundred:	Blackbourn	
Union house:	Onehouse	
Deanery 2000:	Ixworth	

8 miles NW of Stowmarket between Hunston & Walsham le Willows. The church is located on The Street in the village centre. O.S. grid ref: TL 989690
Post Code: IP31 3DH

As you walk round the outside of the church notice the carving of tools on the south-east buttress. Just before you enter the south porch, glance up and on the left you will see St George, and on the right the dragon carved into the spandrels. The entrance door has the original lock. The majority of the church is 15th c. but inside you will find a late 13th c. piscina in the chancel, an early 14th c. piscina in the south aisle next to a window sill sedilia, and a late 14th c. font, all indicating that the church is in all probability a rebuild. Above, the roof has angels looking down from the hammerbeams. Some of the tie-beams are inscribed with the names of the churchwardens and dated 1703. The iron-bound, triple lock, parish chest is on display, as is the old bier.

BARDWELL

		8 miles NE of Bury St
Dedication:	Sts Peter & Paul	Edmunds, between Stanton
No of Bells:	6	& Ixworth Thorpe: east off
Deanery 1836:	Blackbourn	the A143 at Stanton to School
Hundred:	Blackbourn	Lane & Church Street.
Union house:	Bury St Edmunds	O.S. grid ref: TL 941736
Deanery 2000:	Ixworth	Post Code: IP31 1AH

Very difficult to photograph, now that the trees surrounding it are matured. It is unfortunate the architectural beauty cannot be fully appreciated. An historical church with things of great interest never-the-less. There is a glass window representing the benefactor, Sir William Berdewell (1367 - 1434). He paid for the nave roof and the porch which bear his arms. The nave roof is a hammerbeam and arch braced construction and still bears some of the original paintwork. The church was restored in 1853 and a number of wall paintings were discovered including a doom over the chancel arch. There are memorials to the Read and Berdewell family. Oddly, each pier either side of the chancel arch is pierced with a squint. This is not unknown, but it is unusual. The Arms are Hanoverian and are of George II.

9

BARNARDISTON

Dedication: All Saints
No of Bells: 5
Deanery 1836: Clare
Hundred: Risbridge
Union house: Haverhill
Deanery 2000: Clare

4 miles NE of Haverhill between Haverhill & Stradishall: turn off the A143 into village and take first right.
O.S. grid ref: TL 711487
Post Code: CB9 7TL

Above the lovely 14th c. north door one can still see evidence of the old porch roof. Stone tracery and pinnacles remain, but mean little on their own. The later porch is a much taller structure than the original must have been. Within the porch there is a stoup. On the north of the nave is a square turret containing the stairs to the rood loft. Outside on the south buttress of the nave you will find 2 scratch dials, the upper of which seems to bear a date in Roman numerals. There are two pre-reformation bells in the tower. The headstock on one is dated 1622. There is a 15th c. screen and the 14th c. font has only quatrefoils for decoration. The church still retains the frame of the hour-glass stand, and nearby is the Jacobean pulpit.

BARNHAM ST GREGORY

Dedication:	St Gregory	
No of Bells:	4	
Deanery 1836:	Blackbourn	
Hundred:	Blackbourn	
Union house:	Thetford	
Deanery 2000:	Ixworth	

2 miles S of Thetford between Elveden & Euston: situated on The Street in the village centre. Just off the A134.

O.S. grid ref: TL 871792

Post Code: IP24 7NJ

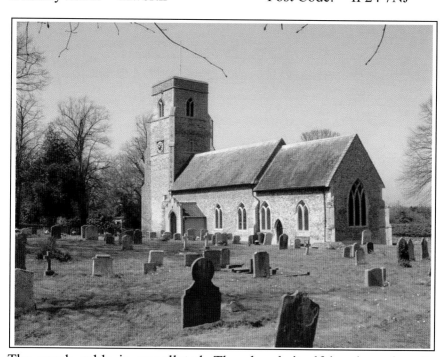

The porch gable is crenellated. The church itself has been heavily restored and has little of any interest to the architect or the historian. H. Munro Cautley writes only two lines, but points out that the chancel contains a 13th c. piscina and is a fine example 'with engaged columns to jambs and moulded arch with unusual cusping'. The 13th c. font is contemporary with the piscina. Cautley also remarks on the 'plain Stuart holy table, a late 16th c. chair and the very uncommon Royal Arms of William III'. I cannot disagree but there is more to this church than Cautley suggests. The church is nicely situated and well maintained. The clock on the markedly stepped tower gave the correct time, and the church is normally open, for which in my view, the P.C.C. deserves a pat on the back.

BARNHAM St Martin

Dedication:	St Martin
No of Bells:	(2)
Deanery 1836:	Blackbourn
Hundred:	Blackbourn
Union house:	Thetford
Deanery 2000:	Ixworth

2 miles S of Thetford between Elveden & Euston: from the A134 take 1st left into Mill Lane, follow 200 yds to St Martin's Meadow.
O.S. grid ref: TL 868793
Post Code: IP24 2NA

A short distance away from St Gregory's are the ivy-clad ruins of St Martin's church which was built about 800 years ago. Only the tower remains above ground and that has lost its top and is sliced down the middle. Once a proud church, it had a peal of two bells which were sold in 1682. The parishes of St. Martin and St. Gregory were consolidated in 1639. The church was completely abandoned about this time, but the name of St. Martin is remembered in road and street names in the parish. These remains of the tower stand in the back garden of a row of cottages. If you do want to visit and see the remains for yourself, please ask first. The picture on the left is mine, but the one on the right is circa 1930 by an unknown photographer to whom we owe our gratitude.

BARNINGHAM *****
Dedication:	St Andrew
No of Bells:	3
Deanery 1836:	Blackbourn
Hundred:	Blackbourn
Union house:	Thetford
Deanery 2000:	Ixworth

7 miles SE of Thetford
between Coney Weston &
Hepworth: from the B1111
(Stanton Road) left at
crossways & follow.
O.S. grid ref: TL 967768
Post Code: IP31 1DE

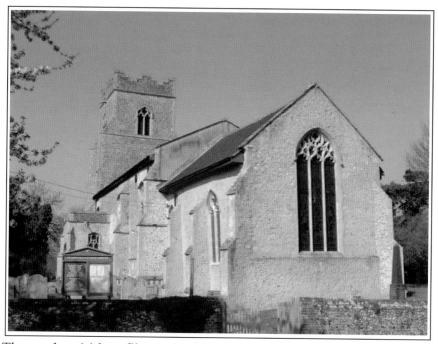

The modest 14th c. flint and rubble built church is somewhat drab on the outside and the brightest thing in view is the Church notice board. Inside, it is a different matter altogether. The stoup in the porch has a small basket of flowers to greet the visitor. The carved woodwork is wonderful, the 29 benches are carved, back, front and ends with poppyheads and birds, lions, pelicans, monkeys, even a pig in a pulpit, (a post-Reformation reference to the Pope). The rood screen is fantastic, with much of the original gilding still visible, although sadly it was varnished in 1933 and is now beyond proper restoration. The pulpit, back and sounding board are all late 17th c.. When I visited, the rood stairs were strewn with flowers, as was the font base. There is a lovely atmosphere in this super little church.

BARROW

Dedication:	All Saints
No of Bells:	5
Deanery 1836:	Thingoe
Hundred:	Thingoe
Union house:	Bury St Edmunds
Deanery 2000:	Thingoe

6 miles W of Bury St Edmunds, between Little Saxham & Higham: from The Street, head north and into Church Road & follow. O.S. grid ref: TL 760646 Post Code: IP29 5BA

In the north wall of the nave is a Norman slit window retaining traces of painted figures, giving a hint to the date of the building. Although restored it retains many of the original features. The 15th c. octagonal font is adorned with painted shields on each of the faces. There is a 14th c. tomb with a pedimented canopy and a sedilia and piscina attached. The second double-drain piscina with central column has a triple-arched sedilia of the same period, although the latter has been heavily restored. The bench ends are old and crudely carved but some of the poppyheads and arm rests are quite grotesque with their strange hairstyles and Derby-style hats. On the north wall of the sanctuary is an Easter sepulchre tomb with some nice brasses and a lengthy inscription to Sir Clement Heigham (1570).

BARTON MILLS

Dedication:	St Mary
No of Bells:	3
Deanery 1836:	Fordham
Hundred:	Lackford
Union house:	Mildenhall
Deanery 2000:	Mildenhall

1 mile S of Mildenhall between Mildenhall & Worlington: the church is situated on The Street in the village centre.

O.S. grid ref: TL 716738

Post Code: IP28 6AR

The square tower is probably 12th c. as is the west door through it. Some have it, however, to be at least 100 years earlier. North and south aisles have been constructed at some time in the past and caused the clerestory to be a necessary addition; although it has only three windows either side it is quite effective. The double piscina is 14th c. and has a central pillar (the detail of the carving is wearing away). There is quite a large amount of 14th c. glass remaining in the windows thanks to the foresight of someone during Puritan times, who removed and hid it. For me the most interesting thing is the parish chest: cut from a tree trunk, it is mostly iron-bound, is 7 feet long and 2 feet wide by 2 feet deep. Inside it has two compartments each with two locks.

BECK ROW

Dedication:	St John the Evangelist	
No of Bells:	1	
Deanery 1836:	Fordham	
Hundred:	Lackford	
Union house:	Mildenhall	
Deanery 2000:	Mildenhall	

1 mile NW of Mildenhall between Mildenhall & Kenny Hill: turn off the A1101 on to St John's Street, S of the Kings Head. O.S. grid ref: TL 699771 Post Code: IP28 8AA

Beck Row was originally a hamlet of Mildenhall, not a parish; but a church was built in 1876 making it a parish. It was constructed by J.D. Wyatt in pseudo-Early English style; a mixture of red brick and stone that is quite pleasing to the eye, although it does appear to be back to front. H Munro Cautley disapproves of it and calls it 'untutored' (or perhaps simply cheap).   Inside the traditional look continues with the pulpit being pseudo-17th c. supported on octagonal piers. On the west gable there is a bellcote with an attractive broached spire housing a single bell. The lychgate which was constructed to enhance the approach to the church doesn't really help the situation. The grounds are well kept but there is no character. The door was securely barred against visitors and parishioners alike.

BEYTON

Dedication:	All Saints
No of Bells:	1, originally 5
Deanery 1836:	Thedwastre
Hundred:	Thedwastre
Union house:	Onehouse
Deanery 2000:	Lavenham

5 miles E of Bury St Edmunds between Bury St Edmunds & Woolpit: in Church Road more or less centrally in the village.
O.S. grid ref: TL 933628
Post Code: IP28 9AL

The church is unusual in having a Norman round or actually somewhat oval tower that is buttressed. There is only one other in the county, at Ramsholt (E. Suffolk. p. 208) and that is at least 100 years later. The north doorway is Norman. The church is almost completely constructed of flint, with stone used only where necessary. The roofs of both nave and chancel are tiled. There were originally 5 bells but 4 were sold around 1775 to pay for repairs to the church. Inside the church there is little of interest except perhaps a Stuart holy table. Some of the wood carving is well executed but is of no great age. The parish chest, if that is what was intended, is a tool-chest which the carpenter must have left behind. The font has a very plain octagonal bowl and shaft of unembellished stone.

17

BILDESTON

Dedication:	St Mary
No of Bells:	6
Deanery 1836:	Sudbury
Hundred:	Cosford
Union house:	Semer
Deanery 2000:	Hadleigh

6 miles NW of Hadleigh
between Hitcham & Semer:
from the High Street, take
Chapel Lane nr the War
Memorial to Church Road.
O.S. grid ref: TL 985492
Post Code: IP7 7EE

The parish of Bildeston was once famous for its cloth and woven blankets. The church is situated on a hill away from the village and is a grand building with a wonderful clerestory which runs the whole length of the nave and chancel. The base of the tower is 100 years older than the church and has a slender new spire mounted on the wooden belfry. The south-east corner of the tower fell through the nave roof in 1975 and rebuilding was not completed until 1997. The traditional East Anglian style font is badly mutilated but you can still make out the wodewoses, lions and angels. The roof has hammerbeams alternating with tie-beams. There are some crudely carved misericordes among many other items of real interest, including the full story of the tower.

BOXFORD
Dedication:	St Mary	
No of Bells:	8	
Deanery 1836:	Sudbury	
Hundred:	Babergh	
Union house:	Semer	
Deanery 2000:	Sudbury	

6 miles E of Sudbury
between Hadleigh &
Newton: from the A1071
turn into Boxford Lane near
the Old School House.
O.S. grid ref: TL 962404
Post Code: CO10 5DX

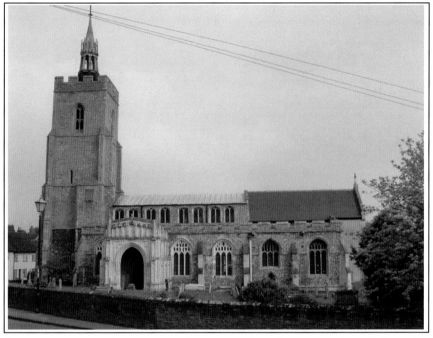

Once seen never forgotten, with the curious lantern spire sitting atop the robust square stone tower. Above the nave is an sixteen-window clerestory and the red tiles on the roof of the chancel add a splash of colour to the otherwise pale colours of nearby plastered houses. The church is mainly 15th c.. The tracery in the windows is of a fine quality. Around the west door you will find carved birds and foliage. The north door has the finest 14th c. wooden porch in the county. The south porch is 15th c., added as an afterthought. The parish chest is of an early date and the 14th c. traceried font has a most unusual 17th c. cover with doors revealing painted texts behind. There are memorials to Elizabeth Hyam who died at 113 and David Birde the rector's son who died suddenly in 1606.

19

BOXTED

Dedication:	All Saints		4½ miles NW of Long
No of Bells:	2		Melford between Stanstead
Deanery 1836:	Sudbury		& Hartest: turn south off
Hundred:	Babergh		The Street near Forge
Union house:	Sudbury		Cottage and follow ½ mile.
Deanery 2000:	Sudbury		O.S. grid ref: TL 824504
			Post Code: IP29 4LN

The open porch with gates rather than doors greet you as you approach the church. On the south-east nave buttress you will find a scratch dial. Inside the church there are two very rare life-size effigies, carved in wood, of William & Alice Poley dated 1579. There is another of Sir John Poley (1638) in the family chapel, carved in alabaster. He is, unusually, depicted in a standing position and wearing an elaborate suit of armour with a helmet at his feet. Next to him is his wife Abigal. Private pews of the Poley family dominate the nave. The pulpit is complete with back and sounding board and is of the Stuart period. The high roof of the nave is 16th c. cambered tie-beam construction. The chancel has a tiled roof of much steeper pitch, suggesting that it was at one time thatched.

BRADFIELD COMBUST

Dedication:	All Saints
No of Bells:	3
Deanery 1836:	Thedwastre
Hundred:	Thedwastre
Union house:	Bury St Edmunds
Deanery 2000:	Lavenham

5½ miles SSE of Bury St Edmunds between Great Welnetham & Cockfield: situated on the A134 near The Manger PH.

O.S. grid ref: TL 892573

Post Code: IP30 0LW

The ancient hall at Bradfield was burnt to the ground during riots in 1327. So much destruction took place that the parish was forever after known as Bradfield Combust (burnt). The western open bell turret is unusual in that it houses three bells. The church is almost all 14th c. but a late 12th c. doorway admits you to the nave which has an arch-braced tie-beam roof with an additional arch-braced collar above. A double cusped piscina in the chancel is next to a very narrow drop window sill sedilia. The font is 12th c. with a heavy cylindrical shaft and a very plain panelled cover. There are two quite outstanding wall paintings opposite the south door of George and the Dragon and St Christopher. A memorial to Arthur Young, LLD, JP (1739) has a quite detailed life history inscribed on the plaque.

BRADFIELD ST CLARE

Dedication:	St Clare	
No of Bells:	3	
Deanery 1836:	Thedwastre	
Hundred:	Thedwastre	
Union house:	Bury St Edmunds	
Deanery 2000:	Lavenham	

6 miles SE of Bury St
Edmunds between Great
Welnetham & Cockfield:
north off Bury Road, which
runs through the village.
O.S. grid ref: TL 909578
Post Code: IP30 0EE

St Clare, after whom the parish is named, was a friend of St Francis of Assisi. This dedication is unique in England. St Clare Hall, now a farmhouse, was once a home to monks from Bury Abbey. The church does not have very much to offer, a home for pigeons in the belfry perhaps. The building is a pleasing conglomerate of local flint, stone and septaria. Lying almost hidden, nestling among pine and some deciduous trees it is unfortunately always locked. I can tell you, however, that the church is 13th c. or at least parts of it are: there is a sepulchral slab built into the chancel wall and a stoup just inside the south door. The holy table is Stuart in date. The chancel roof is arch-braced collar type. Pierced tracery in the Spandrels above the collar break up the austerity of the roof.

22

BRADFIELD ST GEORGE

Dedication:	St George	
No of Bells:	5	
Deanery 1836:	Thedwastre	
Hundred:	Thedwastre	
Union house:	Bury St Edmunds	
Deanery 2000:	Lavenham	

5 miles SE of Bury St Edmunds between Great Welnetham & Felsham: at the western end of Church Road from the village.
O.S. grid ref: TL 906599
Post Code: IP30 0DH

Closely surrounded by trees which create a damp atmosphere, this 600-year-old church is decaying. Over the porch is a sundial which never sees the sun. The west buttresses of the pinnacled and embattled tower have large inscriptions on them relating to their construction and to John Bacon as benefactor. The roof is 16th c. with carved arch-braces and cambered tie-beams, the Spandrels contain tracery decoration. A Norman slit window exists in the south nave wall. The Stuart holy table and pulpit are contemporary with each other. The emulsioned octagonal font is late 14th c. and quite bland. Carved backs to the benches are all different and various creatures replace the usual poppy-heads. I was delighted to see the old bier, which has been restored and is in beautiful condition.

BRAISWORTH

		2 miles S of Eye between
Dedication:	St Mary	Eye & Thorndon: at Old
No of Bells:	1	Church Farm, from
Deanery 1836:	Hartismere	Braisworth Victorian
Hundred:	Hartismere	church head south ½ m.
Union house:	Eye & Wortham	O.S. grid ref: TM 137713
Deanery 2000:	Hartismere	Post Code: IP23 7DS

Standing on the edge of a farmyard, this is all that remains of the Norman church at Braisworth. It was largely demolished about 1855. This was the chancel. The west end was bricked-up to ensure the integrity of the structure as a place of worship, while as much of the material as possible was removed about half a mile up the road to the site of the new church (see next page). A Norman slit window can still be seen in the north wall and a later window and door in the south wall. Inside, the piscina remains with its stone credence shelf. On the floor an effigy of Alexander Newton (1569) in armour. A few stone monuments stand in the graveyard and a broken stone coffin lies nearby. It is surrounded by private land, but the owners were happy to allow me access when I knocked on the farmhouse door.

BRAISWORTH

Dedication: St Mary
No of Bells: 1
Deanery 1836: Hartismere
Hundred: Hartismere
Union house: Ely & Wortham
Deanery 2000: Hartismere

2 miles S of Eye between Eye & Thorndon. Turn off the A140 near Braisworth Lodge (south of the B1117 junction) and follow to end.
O.S. grid ref: TM 133717
Post Code: IP23 7DS

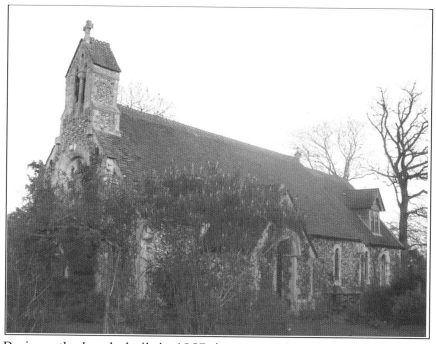

Braisworth church, built in 1857, is now a private dwelling house. It was one of the early conversions and so virtually nothing remains inside. This is the only parish in Suffolk to have two redundant churches. Shipmeadow (E. Suffolk. p. 223) comes a close second with a redundant church and chapel. The single bell can still be seen hanging in the lovely open bell turret. The Norman doorway from the old church is still inside the porch. It is a shame that churches become private houses when we are no longer able to look around them; but at least they are well maintained and the architecture is retained instead of being lost forever. The octofoil window at the west end is most unusual: modern conversions are very restrictive as to what can and cannot be altered inside and out.

BRANDON

Dedication:	St Peter
No of Bells:	6
Deanery 1836:	Fordham
Hundred:	Lackford
Union house:	Thetford
Deanery 2000:	Mildenhall

10 miles NW of Lakenheath between Lakenheath & Mundford, Norfolk. Turn off the A1065 Near Methodist church, into Church Road. O.S. grid ref: TL 777861 Post Code: IP27 0JF

Brandon is an unmistakable church with octagonal conical turrets at the east end of the chancel where one would normally expect to see buttresses. The church is mainly 14th & 15th c. and built almost entirely of flint as one might expect from where Stone Age man mined flint over 5,000 years ago. The north porch is early 16th c. and has inside a rare pillar stoup. The 13th c. font has an octagonal bowl and is supported by eight detached shafts around a central pillar. The south aisle is divided from the nave by a 13th c. pier arcade with moulded bases and caps. The south chapel screens are original 15th c.. Some of the 17th c. poppyheads are interesting and differ from the ordinary. In the north turret which forms part of the sanctuary is an aumbry. Especially worth a lingering look is the east window.

BRENT ELEIGH

Dedication:	St Mary		7 miles NE of Sudbury between Lavenham & Chelsworth. Turn north off the A1141 near The Cock PH & follow to Hall Road.
No of Bells:	3		
Deanery 1836:	Sudbury		
Hundred:	Babergh		
Union house:	Semer		O.S. grid ref: TL 942482
Deanery 2000:	Lavenham		Post Code: CO10 9NP

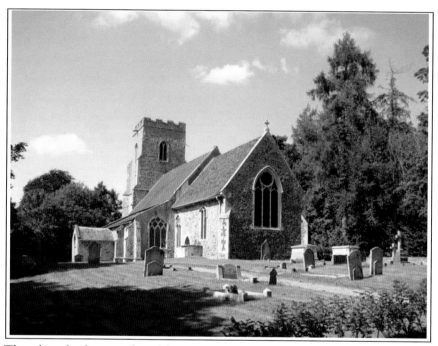

The church sits comfortably on a hill with its embattled square tower and red-tiled roof to the nave and chancel. Outside we see a tomb with a seated skeleton carved into the east end. On the south porch is a scratch dial. The door inside the porch is remarkably 14th c. and still has the original hinges. The 13th c. purbeck font has shallow recessed arcading carved on each of the twelve facets; the shaft is octagonal. There is a 14th c. parclose screen in the south aisle with painted panels. The nave has some 18th c. box pews containing 17th c. benches with crudely carved ends. Wall paintings behind the altar are something one doesn't encounter very often. The chancel contains a rather large monument to "that good man, Mr. Edward Colman, who died in 1739 the last of an ancient family".

27

BRETTENHAM

Dedication:	St Mary
No of Bells:	3
Deanery 1836:	Sudbury
Hundred:	Cosford
Union house:	Semer
Deanery 2000:	Lavenham

7 miles NE of Lavenham between Stowmarket & Lavenham. On three-way junction at the north west side of the parish.
O.S. grid ref: TL 967541
Post Code: IP7 7QR

The church stands very close to where three roads converge. The 14th c. crenulated tower stands to the south of the nave and serves as a porch. The interior of the church is quite dark even on a sunny day. Very little light enters the nave or chancel through the stained glass of the windows. The octagonal font is dated to about the 14th c. with ogee arches and cusped decoration to the bowl and shaft. The cover is a fairly simple octagonal spire with crockets for decoration. The attractive piscina with a cusped ogee arch is not unlike those depicted on the font, and is dated to the same period. It has a buttressed corner pillar in the reveal of the adjacent dropped sill sedilia. The choir lectern is of the Stuart period. Most interesting is that the church uses a 'Basket's Vinegar Bible' of 1716.

BROCKLEY

Dedication:	St Andrew
No of Bells:	3
Deanery 1836:	Thingoe
Hundred:	Thingoe
Union house:	Bury St Edmunds
Deanery 2000:	Thingoe

7 miles S of Bury St Edmunds between Bury St Edmunds & Hartest. Just off the B1066 on Pound Green, very near Brockley Hall. O.S. grid ref: TL 827555 Post Code: IP29 4AQ

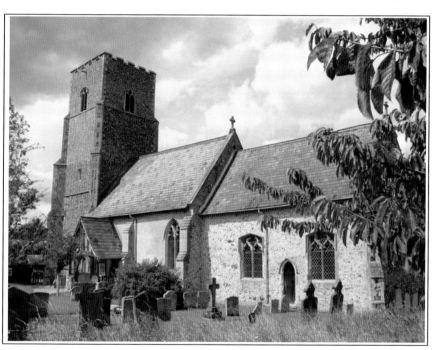

As you approach the church, notice the name of Richardus Coppyng on the base of the tower buttress. He was probably the sponsor of the tower or its restoration at some time. There is also a scratch dial. The little half-timbered porch is 15th c. Close by are some old headstones bearing the symbols of death, very popular at the time. On the door is the original ironwork of the handle and key escutcheon. Beneath the tower are three 15th c. clappers, removed from the bells in 1992. The plain 13th c. octagonal font stands on a central shaft surrounded by eight detached columns. Set into the south wall of the nave is a tomb recess. Above is a cusped ogee arch with a hood mould and a floral finial. The double piscina is early 13th c. with two plain arches and is flanked by the dropped sill sedilia.

BROME

Dedication:	St Mary
No of Bells:	5
Deanery 1836:	Hartismere
Hundred:	Hartismere
Union house:	Eye & Wortham
Deanery 2000:	Hartismere

2 miles N of Eye between Eye & Scole, Norfolk: turn off the A140 at The Swan PH onto the B1077, then turn left in 200 yds, and follow.
O.S. grid ref: TM 145764
Post Code: IP23 8AH

This church is so full of history it deserves much higher recognition than it has. The Norman round tower has a later octagonal top with neat crenellations. But all is not as it seems: almost everything you see is Victorian built. In 1857 and 1863 the old church was almost completely demolished and rebuilt. There is a sketch of the church as it was in about 1850 in the nave. The original styles of construction seem to have been faithfully followed, with most periods represented. The lovely early font was saved from the earlier church. The stone reredos, altar rails, pulpit piscina and sedilia are all the work of James Williams an Ipswich sculptor and stone mason. What is most impressive here though are the effigies and monuments to the Cornwallis or Cornwaleis family. Definitely worth a visit!

BURES

		5 miles S of Sudbury
Dedication:	St Mary	between Sudbury &
No of Bells:	6	Colchester, Essex: within
Deanery 1836:	Sudbury	50 yds of the Swan PH &
Hundred:	Babergh/Hinckford, Essex	the Essex border.
Union house:	Sudbury	O.S. grid ref: TL 906340
Deanery 2000:	Sudbury	Post Code: CO8 5AD

Sitting on the Suffolk / Essex border this interesting church seems to suffer from local apathy. Beautiful monuments are half-hidden by paraphernalia when they should be on display. In the north face of the tower is a pedimented canopy beneath which is a tomb recess. The 650-year-old north porch is half timbered with a tiled roof. The south porch is 16th c. red brick with an elaborate crow-step gable, crenellations and various monochrome designs. Inside is an unusual carved stoup. The 15th c. font has painted armorial shields held by angels around the octagonal bowl. Resting on its window sill tomb is a 14th c. wooden Cornard effigy but who it represents is uncertain. Another monument, to William and Elizabeth Waldergrave, is very pleasing but the obituary is against the wall and can easily be missed.

BURGATE

		4 miles NW of Eye between
Dedication:	St Mary	Wortham & Mellis:
No of Bells:	5	midway between the above
Deanery 1836:	Hartismere	parishes, turn west near Hill
Hundred:	Hartismere	House and follow.
Union house:	Eye & Wortham	O.S. grid ref: TM 083756
Deanery 2000:	Hartismere	Post Code: IP22 1QE

The 14th c. tower dominates the village which supposedly gets its name by being the parish where King Edmund's body rested overnight before continuing the journey to Bury St Edmunds. Most of the church is from the 14th c. but Victorian restoration has taken its toll on the character of the interior. There is a large altar tomb with brasses to Sir William de Burgate in the centre of the chancel. The stout 14th c. font is a typical East Anglian type. The roof is continuous from nave to chancel with some quite eye-catching decorative carving. Also 14th c. is the old parish chest where some painted figures can still just be recognized. The poppy-head carvings on the benches are unusually large and the square pulpit is also well carved. The Royal Arms are of George II dated 1735.

BURY ST EDMUNDS

Dedication:	St James	
No of Bells:	10	
Deanery 1836:	Bury St Edmunds	
Hundred:	Bury St Edmunds	
Union house:	College Street	
Deanery 2000:	Thingoe	

16 miles N of Sudbury between Newmarket & Stowmarket: Situated in Angel Hill near the Abbey Gardens.

O.S. grid ref: TL 855641

Post Code: IP33 1QU

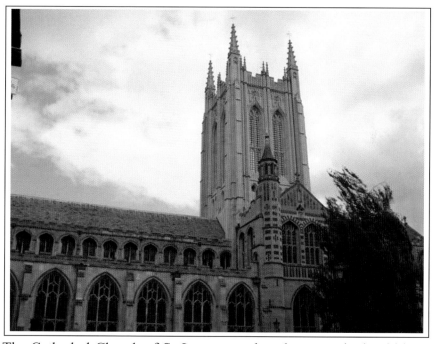

The Cathedral Church of St James now has the tower it should have had when it was first built in the early 16th c. The whole building was restored in the 19th c. and very little remains of the original structure the pier arcade being one of the few exceptions along with some of the 16th c. timbers in the roofs of the aisles. Inside the Cathedral the opulence of the church is blatantly apparent. The font and font cover are covered in gold leaf and garish in appearance. The pulpit has a sounding-board suspended above it. The beauty in this edifice lies in the monuments which are all round the walls and set into the floor. There are extravagances everywhere and money was apparently no object. Guided tours are available, and bookings for groups can be made by telephoning 01284 754933.

BURY ST EDMUNDS

Dedication:	St John	16 miles N of Sudbury between Newmarket & Stowmarket: situated in St John's Street, 500 yards north of Angel Hill.
No of Bells:	1	
Deanery 1836:	Bury St Edmunds	
Hundred:	Bury St Edmunds	
Union house:	College Street	O.S. grid ref: TL 852646
Deanery 2000:	Thingoe	Post Code: IP33 1SN

Built in 1841 of white brick with a magnificent spire, 178 feet tall. Struck by lightening in 1871 and rebuilt a year later. At the corners of each stage of the tower are turrets with conical spires. If it were not for the saving grace of the tower the rest of the building could easily be mistaken for a Victorian village hall (with an attempt at the Early English style). Externally the church building has little of interest. Internally the story is a familiar one. The church was endowed by the Marquis of Bristol and quite naturally is fitted out in a Victorian fashion. The stone reredos is ugly and the carving crudely executed. It is probably worth having a look around, if only to form your own impressions. The church was designed by W. Ranger of London who in my view should have stayed there.

BURY ST EDMUNDS

Dedication:	St Mary
No of Bells:	8
Deanery 1836:	Bury St Edmunds
Hundred:	Bury St Edmunds
Union house:	College Street
Deanery 2000:	Thingoe

16 miles N of Sudbury between Newmarket & Stowmarket: at the junction of Crown Street & Honey Hill. South from Angel Hill. O.S. grid ref: TL 856639 Post Code: IP33 1RT

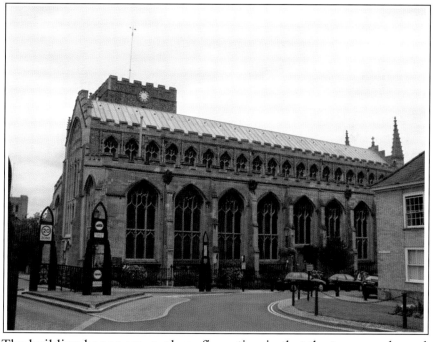

The building has an unusual configuration in that the tower and porch are on the north side. The site upon which the church was built left the builders with no choice. The building was begun in the 15th c. and the single hammerbeams alternate with arch-braced principals. Grotesques, angels, unicorns, dragons and other creatures look down upon the visitor. The eastern bay of the south aisle is a chantry where lies the body of John Baret (1467). Other noteworthy names are Sir Wm. Carewe (1501) and Sir Robert Drury (1536). To me this church is far more interesting architecturally, and historically than the Cathedral, only a door or two away. It is simpler, more modest, and far more people friendly with an atmosphere that is more pleasant and less commercial in character.

BURY ST EDMUNDS

Dedication:	St Peter	16 miles N of Sudbury between Newmarket & Stowmarket: situated in Hospital Road off Horringer Road & Out Westgate.
No of Bells:	1	
Deanery 1836:	Bury St Edmunds	
Hundred:	Bury St Edmunds	
Union house:	College Street	O.S. grid ref: TL 851638
Deanery 2000:	Thingoe	Post Code: IP33 3JT

Built in the 1850's and recently modernised it is, like some other churches in Bury, locked against the visitor. This is a shame because visitors come from hundreds of miles to seek the history of their forebears. Locked churches do not deserve to survive; they ask for donations but leave us standing outside. Our heritage is secreted from us, and to what end? Bury St Edmunds is an historical treasure, greater even than Ipswich or any other part of the county. A locked church is no benefit to man or God. The tourist office in Angel Hill does its best but the short-sightedness of those responsible for the Christian welfare of the community is causing ill feeling and hindering the hard work of others. This is an attractive church with a lovely broached spire, but I didn't find a Christian welcome here.

BUXHALL

Dedication:	St Mary
No of Bells:	6
Deanery 1836:	Stow
Hundred:	Stow
Union house:	Onehouse
Deanery 2000:	Stowmarket

3 miles W of Stowmarket between Stowmarket & Rattlesden: from the B1115 in Gt Finborough turn west into Brettenham Road.
O.S. grid ref: TM 003576
Post Code: IP14 3DJ

This very substantial church was built in the 14th c. and although it was later rendered in cement the work was expertly done and has aged well. There is a scratch dial on the nave buttress. The octagonal font is contemporary with the building of the church and is decorated with cusped and crocketted pediments on each face. The fine double piscina is decorated in a similar manner to the font and could possibly be the work of the same hand. The sedilia utilises a 13th c. sepulchral slab with a cross as a seat. The roof of the chancel is dated J.H.1656 F.G. - T.C. I believe the nave roof to be earlier. There are two benches in the chancel where the craftsmanship of the carpenter deserves praise. Sir William Coppinger was born here in 1512. He was later to become Lord Mayor of London.

CAVENDISH

Dedication:	St Mary
No of Bells:	6
Deanery 1836:	Sudbury
Hundred:	Babergh
Union house:	Sudbury
Deanery 2000:	Clare

6 miles NW of Sudbury between Glemsford & Clare: unmissable, behind 'The George Hotel' on the Green in the village centre.

O.S. grid ref: TL 805465

Post Code: CO10 8AZ

Cavendish church can easily be recognised by the unusual bell framework above the parapet of the turret. Early parts of this lovely church and tower date back to the 14th c. but over the centuries it has been extended. The south porch is part of the original construction. A century later the clerestory was added. The 15th c. octagonal font has mutilated evangelistic emblems, still showing signs of paintwork. Up in the nave roof arch-braced and cambered tie-beams have carved spandrels. The chancel has a barrel roof, the easternmost part of which has been painted. The piscina is fairly plain but the carving above the arch is very elaborate. The eagle lectern is original 15th c. There is a nice altar tomb to Sir George Colt (1570) and his wife. Plenty more to see here, don't forget your camera.

CAVENHAM

Dedication:	St Andrew
No of Bells:	3
Deanery 1836:	Fordham
Hundred:	Lackford
Union house:	Mildenhall
Deanery 2000:	Mildenhall

6 miles NW of Bury St Edmunds between Risby & Tuddenham: at the southern end of The Street opposite Cavenham Park.

O.S. grid ref: TL 762699
Post Code: IP28 6DA

From the road take a good look at the west face of the tower and you will notice a weather mould which once protected a roof. Was the tower once central? It would certainly seem so, but more likely is that the west porch was two-storey and extended as high as the present roof. There is a window looking into the tower which seems to confirm the theory. There is still some very old ironwork on the west door. There are two scratch dials. The south porch now leads us into the 14th c. church, in many ways quite original. Very little has been discarded and it is a pleasure to enjoy the church as it has been for about 600 years. The 14th c. piscina is crudely decorated and there is an aumbry or what may have been a reliquary recess in the north wall of the sanctuary. The old holy table is probably late Stuart.

CHEDBURGH

Dedication:	All Saints	
No of Bells:	1	
Deanery 1836:	Clare	
Hundred:	Risbridge	
Union house:	Bury St Edmunds	
Deanery 2000:	Clare	

6 miles SW of Bury St Edmunds between Horringer & Wickhambrook: on the side of the A143, Bury Road at the east of the village. O.S. grid ref: TL 796574
Post Code: IP29 4US

You either accept it or you hate it. It was largely rebuilt in the reign of Victoria and much of it is white brick. Only part of the nave is 13th c., the rest having been used as hardcore for local roads. But despite being permanently locked and remote from the parish it serves I quite like certain aspects of it. The north tower is well proportioned and the spire is neat (and a good landmark). Some of the original 14th c. windows have been salvaged and re-used, with some of the glass remaining within them. Being unable to enter, I can tell you little about the interior and what delights there may be in store. H. Munro Cautley tells us that four traceried panels of the old rood screen have been preserved and incorporated into the modern woodwork. A church beautifully situated, but sadly dejected.

CHELSWORTH

Dedication:	All Saints
No of Bells:	1
Deanery 1836:	Sudbury
Hundred:	Cosford
Union house:	Semer
Deanery 2000:	Lavenham

5 miles NW of Hadleigh between Monks Eleigh & Bildeston: on a bend in the B1115 as it passes through the village, near the Grange O.S. grid ref: TL 980479 Post Code: IP7 7HX

Chelsworth's 14th c. church is very recognisable as it is shabby cream-coloured on the north side. It appears to be almost derelict, but inside it is alive and vibrant. One of the first things that catches the eye is a doom painting over the chancel arch. Although this is faded and damaged through being whitewashed over, it is still possible to make out most of the features. At one time there was a north chapel in the chancel but this has been removed; only the corbels for the roof remain. In the north aisle there is a fine tomb set into the wall. The decorative detail of the canopy is very fine. It is thought to be the tomb of Sir John de Philibert (1359). The 14th c. octagonal font has crocketted and cusped pediments on each of the faces of the bowl and a plain octagonal shaft. The iron-bound rounded-top chest is 14th c.

CHEVINGTON

Dedication: All Saints
No of Bells: 5
Deanery 1836: Thingoe
Hundred: Thingoe
Union house: Bury St Edmunds
Deanery 2000: Thingoe

5 miles SW of Bury St Edmunds between Ousden & Whepstead: turn north at Broad Green and follow, bear right at the junction.
O.S. grid ref: TL 788601
Post Code: IP29 5QH

Built in the 13th c. by the Anglo-Normans but altered and restored by Victorian craftsmen. The half-timbered south porch protects a beautiful 12th c. Norman doorway with engaged columns and modestly decorated arch. The nave roof is arch-braced with cambered tie beams. The octagonal 15th c. font is badly mutilated and the buttressed shaft is in an even worse state. The parish chest is superbly carved with monkeys, eagles and a dragon at one end of the front. The rest has representations of many creatures among tracery. The bench ends and finials are really worthy of close examination with various carvings, some of angels playing musical instruments. The backs of the benches too are carved, possibly utilised when the rood screen was dismantled. The Royal Arms are those of George I.

CHILTON

Dedication:	St Mary
No of Bells:	1
Deanery 1836:	Sudbury
Hundred:	Babergh
Union house:	Sudbury
Deanery 2000:	Sudbury

1 mile from Sudbury town centre on the NE outskirts: on the edge of the Industrial Estate in Churchfield Road.

O.S. grid ref: TL 889422
Post Code: CO10 2YA

This church is regarded as remote and is always locked, although as the notice says there is nothing of value inside and to call the keyholder's number for the key. (Better by far than no keyholder and no telephone to call). The church is 15th c and surrounded by trees. The brick tower is later and sits at the west of the nave. The crenellations are well defined and a slender pinnacle adorns each corner. The font is of panelled design and dates back to the 15th c.. The Crane chapel contains many monuments, the one to Sir Robert Crane (1624) and his two wives being the most outstanding. Other earlier members of the Crane family are here too in splendid altar tombs. One has the 'SS' emblem on his collar, another has a money bag fastened to his waist to demonstrate his wealth. Hoping to take it with him perhaps!

CLARE

Dedication: Sts Peter & Paul
No of Bells: 8 (heaviest peal in Suffolk)
Deanery 1836: Clare
Hundred: Risbridge
Union house: Haverhill
Deanery 2000: Clare

7 miles NW of Sudbury between Haverhill & Long Melford: unmissable on the A1092 in the centre of the parish in Church Street.
O.S. grid ref: TL 769454
Post Code: CO10 8PB

Clare church sits prominently in the centre of the parish, not far from The Castle. The tower base is 13th c. and the oldest part of the building. The porches are 14th c.. Extensive building work in the 15th c. gave the church the façade you see today. Much Roman brick has been incorporated into the fabric. Between the nave and chancel are turret stairs which continue above the roof line. Externally it seems a hotch-potch of add-ons. Internally it is delightful. The aisle pillars have the octagonal bases which were added to raise the height of the nave. On entering, the eye is drawn to an unusual gallery pew for the Barker family, beneath which is the mediaeval parish chest. The tracery woodwork on the chantry pew, close by, is exceptionally fine. Much of the furniture is Jacobean and intricately carved.

COCKFIELD

Dedication: St Peter
No of Bells: 6
Deanery 1836: Sudbury
Hundred: Babergh
Union house: Semer
Deanery 2000: Lavenham

7 miles SE of Bury St
Edmunds between Bury &
Lavenham: turn off the
A1141 to Cockfield then
north into Church Lane.
O.S. grid ref: TL 903550
Post Code: IP30 0LA

The cottages near the church gate are 14th c., older than some parts of the church. The tower with chequered parapet is 15th c. but parts of the church dates from the 12th c.. Although not as obvious as some, the nave has a clerestory above, making the interior nice and light. The roof of the nave has tie beams and kingposts. There are two fonts. The old 14th c. one has been re-cut to be almost plain and bears the cover. The new one is crisp, although the design is uninteresting. There is a lovely 14th c. Easter sepulchre in the wall with a triple traceried canopy. A small niche beneath a window from 200 years earlier with a cusped head is the oldest thing you will see here. A memorial to James Harvey (1723) forms part of a grander memorial to the Harvey family.

COMBS

Dedication:	St Mary
No of Bells:	4
Deanery 1836:	Stow
Hundred:	Stow
Union house:	Onehouse
Deanery 2000:	Stowmarket

1 mile S of Stowmarket between Stowmarket & Little Finborough: north west of the parish in Church Road, near Combs Hall.
O.S. grid ref: TM 051569
Post Code: IP14 2EH

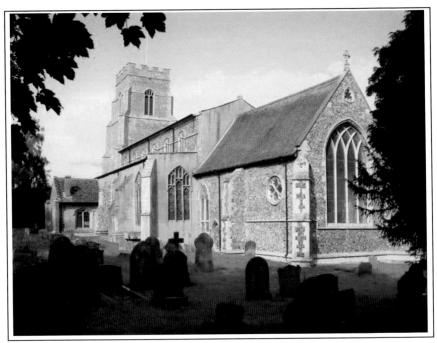

This is a lovely example of a Suffolk church. It has one or two peculiarities about it too. The base of the tower has a doorway north and south to allow processions to walk round the church without leaving consecrated ground. The unused south porch is built of red brick. Later additions have been added to the building which is 14th c., the nave roof for example, which had to be reconstructed after threatening to spread. The font is late 14th c. contemporary with the building of the church. Retouched paintings can be seen on the lower part of the rood screen. The pulpit and holy table are of the Stuart period. A relatively simple parish chest bears the date 1599. I do not often mention the window glass but some really fine glass can be seen here, particularly in the window of the south aisle.

CONEY WESTON

Dedication:	St Mary	
No of Bells:	1	
Deanery 1836:	Blackbourn	
Hundred:	Blackbourn	
Union house:	Thetford	
Deanery 2000:	Ixworth	

6 miles SE of Thetford
between Hopton All Saints
& Sapiston: well east of the
village on the Hopton Road,
past Coney Weston Hall.
O.S. grid ref: TL 971783
Post Code: IP31 1HQ

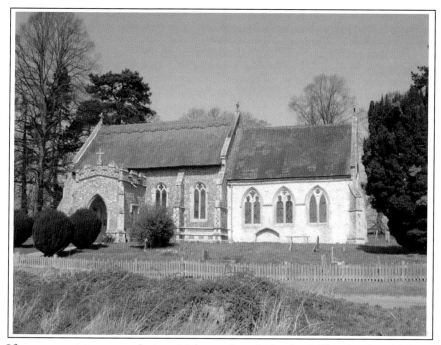

If you want to see what a 14th c. church looked like in the 14th c., look no further than Coney Weston. There is no tower, nor has there ever been a tower. Inside the attractive 14th c. porch is a stoup, now obstructed with a welcome notice. Hidden away in a corner is the octagonal 13th c. font with panels which are carved with unusual designs. Hidden behind a heater and gas bottles, I found two niches each with delightful paintings of angels. The piscina in the chancel is 14th c. with a corner pillar flanked by sedilia on two levels, the height of which indicated that the chancel floor had been raised at some time since sedilia went out of use. It is a beautiful little church but why do things such as heaters, tables and bookshelves have to obscure the things the visitor comes to see. If you've got it, flaunt it!

COTTON

Dedication:	St Andrew	
No of Bells:	5	
Deanery 1836:	Hartismere	
Hundred:	Hartismere	
Union house:	Eye & Wortham	
Deanery 2000:	Stowmarket	

5 miles N of Stowmarket between Mendlesham & Bacton: east off the B1113 into Parkers Road, Cock Road & to Church Road. O.S. grid ref: TM 070669 Post Code: IP14 4RA

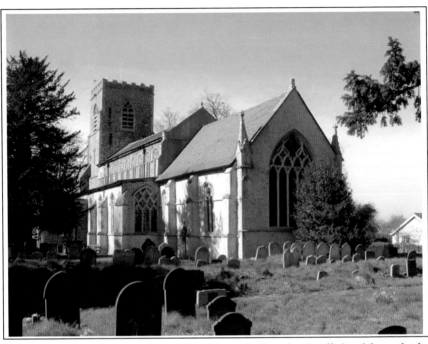

Cotton was immortalised in Pip Wright's book 'Lydia', although the church, which has many interesting features, was not a strong element in the story. The tower has enormous buttresses almost 5 feet wide which stand at right-angles to the face of the tower. The western arch is uncommonly lofty. At the opposite end of the church the pinnacles which rise from the east corners are elegantly crocketted with shallow niches below. The south porch protects the lovely 14th c. door, with three engaged columns each side and decorated arch above. The nave, made lofty by the clerestory, has a superb double hammerbeam roof. The eastern bay is panelled and forms a canopy of honour to the non-existent rood. The pulpit, holy table and rails are Stuart. One bench has oddly detailed carving. The piscina is 14th c.

COWLINGE

Dedication:	St Margaret
No of Bells:	5
Deanery 1836:	Clare
Hundred:	Risbridge
Union house:	Haverhill
Deanery 2000:	Clare

10 miles SW of Bury St Edmunds: between Great Bradley & Wickhambrook, just off Newmarket Road near Green Man House.
O.S. grid ref: TL 718549
Post Code: CB8 9QA

This is an interesting little church, but it has suffered at the hands of restorers and is now (2008) undergoing extensive repairs to the roof of the south aisle. The plain brick-built tower is 18th c. and mars the appearance of the church. Inside the church the 14th c. roof seems to catch the eye, with its kingposts and tie-beams. The doom painting over the chancel arch depicts St Michael weighing the souls of the dead. There is a poor example of a parclose screen in the south aisle. The octagonal font is early 15th c.: the bowl has simple geometric designs, the shaft and base are also octagonal. The 6 ft. parish chest is simple in its construction. There is a small brass memorial plaque to Robert Higham (1571) and to Margaret, his wife (1599). The Royal Arms of George II are dated 1731.

CREETING

Dedication:	St Peter
No of Bells:	3
Deanery 1836:	Stow
Hundred:	Stow
Union house:	Onehouse
Deanery 2000:	Bosmere

2½ miles SE of Stowmarket: between Stowmarket & Needham Mkt. From the village cross over the A14 into Pound Road & follow. O.S. grid ref: TM 080576
Post Code: IP6 8QJ

Creeting St Peter church is separated from the parish by the A14 trunk road. Set in a lovely secluded part of the Suffolk countryside, this charming little church dates back to the 12th c.. The building was rescued from dereliction in the 19th c.. Victorian renovations have been well executed and its charm retained. Almost every style of architectural period is represented in the type of window. The unique painting of St Christopher is very clear, although only the upper part remains. A ribbon scroll still carries the text 'Whoever looks at the picture of St Christopher shall assuredly on that day be burdened with no weariness'. The font is a traditional East Anglian type. The heptagonal pulpit is most unusual and is almost 600 years old. The holy table is quite small and from the Stuart period.

		4 miles N of Bury St
CULFORD		Edmunds: between West
Dedication:	St Mary	Stow & Ingham. West on
No of Bells:	1	B1106 into Culford Park
Deanery 1836:	Blackbourn	School entrance, & follow.
Hundred:	Blackbourn	O.S. grid ref: TL 833703
Union house:	Bury St Edmunds	Post Code: IP28 6TU
Deanery 2000:	Thingoe	

Sitting in the beautiful grounds of Culford Park and Hall, not far from the River Lark, this is a pleasant little church with important connections. The original church was designed and built by Sir Stephen Fox, whose daughter married the third Lord Cornwallis. This well proportioned Victorian edifice was built in traditional materials and was consecrated in 1865. Fortunately the importance of the monuments were recognised and have been saved and well cared for. Nathaniel Bacon (1627), Lady Jane Bacon (1654) and her five grand-children are among the famous names immortalised here. The reredos is a highly crafted construction and is a memorial to the Earl of Cadogan (1909). The north aisle was built to house the memorial to the Countess of Cadogan (1907).

DALHAM

Dedication:	St Mary
No of Bells:	5
Deanery 1836:	Clare
Hundred:	Risbridge
Union house:	Exning
Deanery 2000:	Mildenhall

5 miles E of Newmarket between Gazely & Lidgate. From the B1085 turn north & take right fork to the church.
O.S. grid ref: TL 724625
Post Code: CB8 8TB

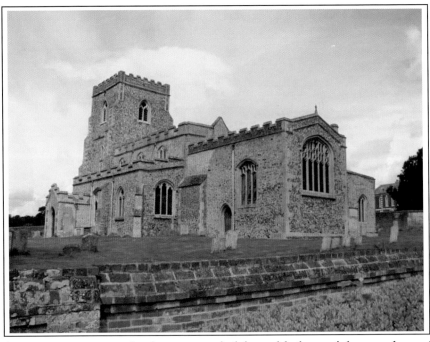

A squat tower seemingly surrounded by added-on aisles, a chancel and north transept; with fine crenellations, even on the 14th c. porch. The church was re-edified in 1625 and a large board at the west end of the nave tells the full story. Around the top are words of advice to the parishioners. Sir Martin Stuteville (1631) was responsible for the work and his tomb is in the sanctuary. There was once a spire above the tower but the gale that affected all England the night Oliver Cromwell died saw its demise. The lower part of the 15th c. rood screen remains and still bears much of its original colouring. Some of the wall paintings are noteworthy. Inside the church the benches are carved with a menagerie of creatures. Colonel Francis Rhodes (1905) brother of Cecil is interred here. Worthy of an hour of your time.

DENHAM

Dedication:	St Mary	
No of Bells:	1	
Deanery 1836:	Thingoe	
Hundred:	Risbridge	
Union house:	Bury St Edmunds	
Deanery 2000:	Thingoe	

7 miles SW of Bury St Edmunds: between Ousden & Barrow, situated near Denham Hall south west of Barrow.
O.S. grid ref: TL 755618
Post Code: IP29 5EF

From outside you would not give this church a second glance. Your attention may be turned to nearby Denham Castle, once a Norman stronghold amid the resident Saxons. It would be a shame not to examine the church closer, for in the red-brick chapel north of the chancel you will find the beautiful tomb of Edward Lewkenor (1605) and his wife Susan, who died of smallpox. They are accompanied by their two sons and six daughters, all kneeling beneath an enormous canopy. Lying close by, carved in white marble and dressed in full armour, is their grandson, also Edward, who was the last of the line. He also died of smallpox in 1634. Unfortunately this little church has little else to offer, and with such beautiful monuments to protect, it is usually locked.

DENSTON

Dedication:	St Nicholas
No of Bells:	2
Deanery 1836:	Clare
Hundred:	Risbridge
Union house:	Haverhill
Deanery 2000:	Clare

7 miles NE of Haverhill between Stradishall & Hawkedon: situated on the Denston to Stradishall Road.
O.S. grid ref: TL 760529
Post Code: CB8 8PP

H. Munro Cautley was most impressed with this church, calling it 'probably the most beautiful and interesting in the county.' Who am I to disagree with the great man? It is everything he describes it as. There is a stoup on the outside wall, and a fan vaulted roof on the inside of the porch. Fine arcades line the aisle and chancel, terminating in the lovely east window. The clerestory is magnificent and lofty and the old rood beam still spans the width of the aisle. The mediaeval font is one of the seven sacrament type and is beautifully crisp. At the junction of the walls and roof is the fine carved cornice depicting lions, deer, hounds and hares. The benches too are worthy of close inspection. There are some very famous names buried here and many of the memorials are brass. Worthy of a couple of hours.

DEPDEN

Dedication:	St Mary
No of Bells:	3
Deanery 1836:	Clare
Hundred:	Risbridge
Union house:	Bury St Edmunds
Deanery 2000:	Clare

7 miles SW of Bury St Edmunds:between Chedburgh & Wickhambrook off the A143, take ¼ mile footpath from Beech Hall.
O.S. grid ref: TL 777566
Post Code: IP29 4BU

The buttresses at the east end of the chancel have pinnacles which carry up to the roof-line. They were erected in the 14th c., but serve no real purpose. The shabby looking porch is the vestry and protects the beautiful Norman doorway at the west end of the nave. The 17th c. north porch is a simple structure. Two of the bells are 15th c. as is the tower which is heavily buttressed. The piscina is 14th c. and has a central mullion with a cusped and double arched head. The simple font is comparatively quite late at about 1680.   The benches are notable for their carvings and traceried ends. There are two brass memorials to Lady Anne Jermyn. One depicts her with her first husband and six children, the other with her second husband. The Royal Arms are of William IV and dated 1836.

DRINKSTONE

Dedication:	All Saints
No of Bells:	6
Deanery 1836:	Thedwastre
Hundred:	Thedwastre
Union house:	Onehouse
Deanery 2000:	Lavenham

6½ miles SE of Bury St Edmunds: between Woolpit & Hessett; situated in The Street of the village.

O.S. grid ref: TL 959616

Post Code: IP30 9SX

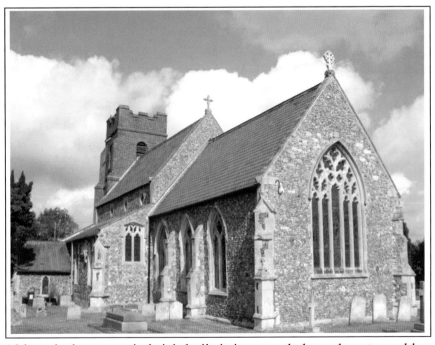

Although the tower is brick-built it is nevertheless almost as old as the rest of the church. Before you enter, take a look at the memorials on the south nave wall. A carved cock is perched on the edge above the one to Simon Cocksedge, a rebus of his name. A little further east are buttresses of an unusual design. Inside the porch is a stoup, a survivor from the 14th c.. The 13th c. font, with its eight detached shafts, suffered badly at the hands of the Puritans. The pulpit rests on the top of an ancient altar tomb, intentionally lowered to accommodate it. The splendid 15th c. screen is the work of a craftsman and bears fine tracery and some original colour on the panels. There is a dropped-sill sedilia which contains a traceried rail that may at one time have been part of the rood loft.

EDWARDSTONE

Dedication:	St Mary
No of Bells:	6
Deanery 1836:	Sudbury
Hundred:	Babergh
Union house:	Semer
Deanery 2000:	Sudbury

4 miles E of Sudbury: between Boxford & Great Waldingfield; turn west off the main road through the village near The Hall.
O.S. grid ref: TL 940420
Post Code: CO10 5PH

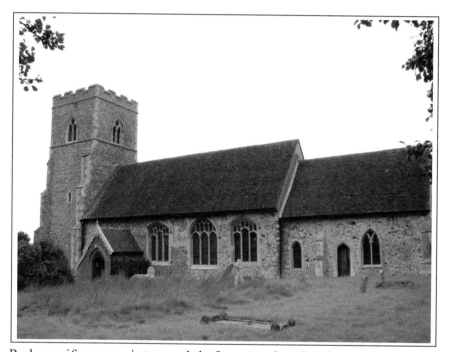

Perhaps, if you are interested; before entering the church take a walk round the churchyard. There is an unusual assortment of cast iron memorials here (the poor man's headstone). Some, unfortunately, had the long-gone name painted on a plain background, others were cast and are more permanent. The 14th c. church contains little of interest but has its good points: the plain octagonal font with its eight detached pillars and 17th c. wooden cover, for example. The fine Jacobean panelled pulpit complete with sounding board also catches the attention. Above, fine crown posts set on cross-beams support the roof. A memorial to Benjamin Brand and his wife Elizabeth and their twelve children who were 'all nursed with her unborrowed milk' is an interesting brass.

ELMSETT

Dedication:	St Peter
No of Bells:	2
Deanery 1836:	Sudbury
Hundred:	Cosford
Union house:	Semer
Deanery 2000:	Hadleigh

4 miles NE of Hadleigh between Whatfield & Burstall; at the eastern end of The Street turn into Manor Road.
O.S. grid ref: TM 058472
Post Code: IP7 6PJ

Well worth a look round although a half-hour will cover all things of interest. There is a scratch dial to find on the chancel window. The porch appears to be older than the church but of course it is not. The 700-year-old gnarled timbers which guard the entrance and the door to the nave are indeed ancient. The late 12th c. square font bowl with a central support and a column at each corner is noteworthy. The cover is 17th c.. The pulpit is well carved and probably Stuart, as are the panels and much of the various pieces of woodwork. Take time to read the tablet below the memorial to Edward Sherland who died in 1609. Once you get used to the v for u and ancient spellings it is a superb epitaph. There is a corner piscina and dropped-sill sedilia. The Royal Arms are those of Queen Anne and are dated 1758.

ELMSWELL

Dedication:	St John the Divine
No of Bells:	5
Deanery 1836:	Blackbourn
Hundred:	Blackbourn
Union house:	Onehouse
Deanery 2000:	Lavenham

5 miles NW of Stowmarket between Stowmarket & Thurston: from the A14 & A1088 you pass the church on the way to the village. O.S. grid ref: TL 982635 Post Code: IP30 9ES

A lovely 14th c. church that is well cared for. Near the south-west corner of the tower is a memorial slab enclosed by a protective cage of wrought iron. There is one other like it at Henham in Essex. On the tower buttresses, Gothic script records some past events or deeds and the fine tracery in the stonework is most unusual and is worthy of closer inspection. The font bowl is octagonal and supported by angels. It has one blank shield, the other seven are decorated. The octagonal shaft is also nicely decorated. The clerestory is hardly noticeable from the outside but admits plenty of light to the inside. The monument to Sir Robert Gardener (1619) complete with a rhinoceros at his feet is enclosed by an old parclose screen. There are some richly carved bench ends with traceried panels.

ELVEDON

		4 miles SW of Thetford,
Dedication:	Sts Andrew & Patrick	Norfolk: between Thetford
No of Bells:	1	& Barton Mills; on the A11
Deanery 1836:	Fordham	as you pass through,
Hundred:	Lackford	opposite the Estate Shop.
Union house:	Mildenhall	O.S. grid ref: TL 822799
Deanery 2000:	Mildenhall	Post Code: IP24 3TL

If you park in the shop car park opposite, take care crossing the road. The church is virtually Victorian and has been expanded beyond reason. The old 14th c. nave has Norman slit windows and niches each side. The chancel also shows signs of the earlier building and has a simple piscina. The sedilia is the sill of a 14th c. window. The north nave and chancel are much later additions to the church as are the cloisters and tower to the south of the church proper. These were all built by Maharajah Duleep Singh and his memorial column is about a mile away by the side of the road to the south. It is all very interesting to the architectural student but holds little or no interest for the historian. It is worth a look round its extravagant interior as it illustrates what all churches must have been like pre-Cromwell.

ERISWELL

Dedication:	St Peter
No of Bells:	?
Deanery 1836:	Fordham
Hundred:	Lackford
Union house:	Mildenhall
Deanery 2000:	Mildenhall

2 miles north of the village: between Lakenheath & Mildenhall; seen from the B1112 in the grounds of Eriswell Hall.

O.S. grid ref: TL 723780

Post Code: IP27 9BH

This was once the parish church of Eriswell but little of it remains today. It was more recently converted to a dovecot in the 18th c. and an etching of it is still in existence. It fell into disuse very early, and the Chapel of Ease at the site of the present church was converted and extended to create a parish church nearer the parish. The chapel was actually in the hamlet of Coclesworth which was later incorporated into Eriswell. The stone and flint of the building was removed to rebuild part of the tower at Lakenheath. Some parts of the old church can still be recognised as such; a nave window with 15th c. tracery almost weathered away and what may be an original buttress on the south east corner. Curiosity value only, I'm afraid.

ERISWELL

Dedication: St Peter
No of Bells: 3
Deanery 1836:   Fordham
Hundred: Lackford
Union house: Mildenhall
Deanery 2000:   Mildenhall

3 miles S of Lakenheath: between Lakenheath & Mildenhall; on a bend in the B1112 on the southern edge of the village.
O.S. grid ref: TL 721807
Post Code: IP27 9AZ

Originally dedicated to St. Laurence as a Chapel of Ease The dedication proved unpopular and is not as commonly used as St Peter, which was transferred from the original church. (see page 61). An interesting building and much of it 14th & 15th c. workmanship. Entry is gained from the north porch and the 14th c. font is immediately noticeable with clustered columns forming the central shaft. The south aisle is almost as large as the main aisle and contains all the usual accoutrements, including a piscina, complete with credence shelf, and an aumbry. There is an earlier 14th c. piscina in the chancel and a sedilia with arm rests. There are some old benches, the carvings on which have been dreadfully mutilated. The screen is nicely carved and is contemporary with the original building work.

EUSTON

Dedication:	St Genevieve
No of Bells:	5
Deanery 1836:	Blackbourn
Hundred:	Blackbourn
Union house:	Thetford
Deanery 2000:	Ixworth

2½ miles SSE of Thetford, Norfolk: between Thetford & Honington; off the A1088 in the grounds of Euston Hall. O.S. grid ref: TL 900784 Post Code: IP24 2QW

A cement-rendered and relatively modern edifice, unusual in its appearance, the slender tower with its corner pinnacles penetrating the skyline. Sitting in the grounds of Euston Hall, home of the Dukes of Grafton, it is not inaccessible but try getting inside! It is locked and secured against all comers. It was built on the foundations of the original building by Henry Bennett, Earl of Arlington, in the style of the original. Not being able to gain access there is not much I can say about it, except to crib from H. Munro Cautley. 'There is much distinguished 17th c. ornamental plasterwork, wainscoting and carving. The furnishings of 1676 include a handsome pulpit ..' Modest memorials to members of the FitzRoys include the one, who was Prime Minister under George III.

EXNING

Dedication:	St Agnes
No of Bells:	5 + 1 clock bell
Deanery 1836:	Fordham
Hundred:	Lackford
Union house:	Exning
Deanery 2000:	Mildenhall

13 miles W of Bury St
Edmunds between Ely,
Cambs & Haverhill on the
A13004, Bury Road,
opposite Rockfield House.
O.S. grid ref: TL 650640
Post Code: CB8 7BT

A Victorian church built in 1886 and commissioned by the Duchess
of Montrose in memory of her husband, William Stuart Stirling
Crawford. It was built by R.H. Carpenter from red brick and stone
and the theme is carried into the interior. The tower cum turret is
unusual and is pleasantly light in appearance. Just above the louvers
in the stone belfry stage are graceful arches, carved in fine detail. The
slender spirelet is delicately crocketted. I like it because it is not
trying to look like something it is not. The interior is lavish with
mosaic and a majolica-tiled dado. The reredos is a beautifully carved
depiction of the Assumption of the BVM by Boehm. Above is a blind
arcade containing six saints within the arches. The whole of the east
wall is tiled in mosaic and is unique in Suffolk. No keyholder.

EXNING

Dedication:	St Martin	
No of Bells:	5 + clock bell	
Deanery 1836:	Clare	
Hundred:	Lackford	
Union house:	Exning	
Deanery 2000:	Mildenhall	

2 miles NW of Newmarket between Fordham & Cambridge, Cambs; on the B1103 as it passes through Exning on Church Street.
O.S. grid ref: TL 621655
Post Code: CB8 7EH

Exning church stands slightly aloof from the street and is partially screened by trees. A curious little clock-bell turret sits atop the 14th c. tower, and a broken stone coffin lies at its base. The church had been over-restored. Thankfully the Victorians merely covered the earlier work and it remained hidden, revealed by more enlightened modern restoration. The age of the church can be further established by the early 14th c. simple arched piscina with a double drain. The pulpit is 18th c. and still has its original back and sounding board. In what is now St Wendreda's chapel, an aumbry, ornamental piscina and double heartshrine were uncovered during restoration in 1972. There is much of interest here, some of it unique and I strongly recommend a visit to what is our most westerly church.

EYE	*****	4 miles SE of Diss, Norfolk
Dedication:	St Peter & St Paul	between Brome & Occold;
No of Bells:	8	easily found, close to the
Deanery 1836:	Hartismere	castle, on the B1117 Hoxne
Hundred:	Hartismere	Road, see also the Guildhall.
Union house:	Eye & Wortham	O.S. grid ref: TM 148737
Deanery 2000:	Hartismere	Post Code: IP23 7BD

This is not the best view of the church but climbing to the top of the Norman castle gives a different viewpoint. The old Guildhall is the timbered building on the left. The tower which dominates the church is 15th c. and has fine flushwork and octagonal buttressing. Arms of the De la Pole family can be seen in a number of locations. The south porch, with its chamber above, is a mess and mars the grandeur of this fine church. It ought to be properly restored. The doorway it protects is early 13th c.. On the porch wall is hung a dole table, and the text above it is worthy of note. The octagonal font is richly carved and bears a fine cover. The most interesting feature, however, is the beautiful rood screen. The loft and rood were restored in 1925 and illustrate perfectly how all rood screens once appeared.

FAKENHAM MAGNA

Dedication:	Sts Peter & Paul	
No of Bells:	3	
Deanery 1836:	Blackbourn	
Hundred:	Blackbourn	
Union house:	Thetford	
Deanery 2000:	Ixworth	

5 miles SSE of Thetford,
Norfolk: between Thetford,
Norfolk & Ixworth; on a
dangerous bend of the
A1088 (Thetford Road).
O.S. grid ref: TL 910766
Post Code: IP24 2QX

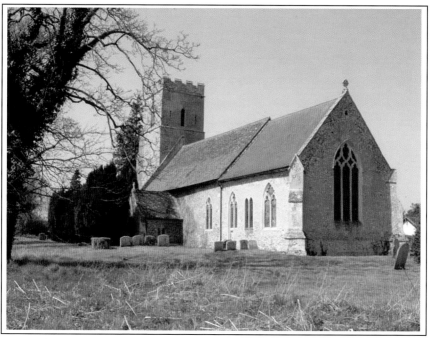

Not to be confused with Fakenham in Norfolk! This is a very old church. As signs of Saxon building methods are clear to see. Long and short quoins are evident in the stonework of the nave. Slit windows, although blocked are still visible in the nave walls. The buttresses at the corner of the chancel are gabled. As you wander round, notice how the churchyard is higher than the base of the church walls, a sure sign of an early structure. Inside the old south porch is a restored stoup, but on the door is an original 14th c. ring-handle on a boss in the form of a mask. The rood screen has been well restored and retains some of the original paintwork. Don't bother looking for Fakenham Parva; it was totally destroyed and incorporated into the Euston estate 300 years ago.

FELSHAM

Dedication:	St Peter
No of Bells:	6
Deanery 1836:	Thedwastre
Hundred:	Thedwastre
Union house:	Onehouse
Deanery 2000:	Lavenham

7 miles of Stowmarket:
between Rattlesden &
Cockfield; in the centre of
the village (Church Road)
opposite Six Bells PH.
O.S. grid ref: TL 946570
Post Code: IP30 0PJ

As you enter the churchyard through the old lych gate note the seats built into the wall. They were cut, I believe, from old headstones. The magnificent 15th c. north porch adorned with superb stone and flint panelled flushwork greets you. There are traces of two scratch dials for you to find. The south aisle is embattled and has a centrally situated porch. The interior has little of architectural or historical interest: suffice to say it has been over-restored. Two windows in the nave are 14th c. and have some old glass set into them. The rest of the glass is modern tinted. The 15th c. font is probably the most interesting and unusual item this church has to offer. The holy table is late 17th c.   Above the chancel arch hang the Royal Arms of George III, dated 1820.

FINNINGHAM

Dedication:	St Bartholomew
No of Bells:	3
Deanery 1836:	Hartismere
Hundred:	Hartismere
Union house:	Eye & Wortham
Deanery 2000:	Ixworth

6 miles SW of Eye:
between Gislingham &
Bacton; just off the B1113
and north of the crossroads,
behind some houses.
O.S. grid ref: TM 066694
Post Code: IP14 4JE

The tower spoils the appearance of this otherwise attractive little church. It has been cement-rendered upwards from the mid-point instead of being properly restored. There is a scratch dial to seek out. The south porch has been restored and is adorned with flint and stone flushwork. Shame about the broken pinnacle; so easily remedied! Inside the church the single hammerbeam and arch-braced collar roof attracts the eye. High on the west wall of the nave the sanctus bell window remains unblocked. The font is late 15th c. and has a traceried bowl and shaft, above which is a lovely, complex, carved mediaeval cover. Some of the benches may have been carved by the same hand, having traceried ends and figures and grotesques on the arm-rests.

FLEMPTON (cum HENGRAVE)
Dedication: St Catherine
No of Bells: 1
Deanery 1836:   Thingoe
Hundred: Thingoe
Union house: Bury St Edmunds
Deanery 2000:   Thingoe

4½ miles NW of Bury St
Edmunds: between Bury St
Edmunds & Icklingham; on
the crossroads of the A1101
near The Greyhound PH.
O.S. grid ref: TL 813699
Post Code: IP28 6BL

Hengrave church is now out of use, the Convent at Hengrave Hall having been sold into private hands (see page 99). About Flempton there is not much to say. Mature trees and Irish Yews adorn the churchyard, but restoration has ripped the heart and soul from the building. The tower has been recently restored (2007). Although it may be practical, the grey slate roof doesn't help the look of the church , giving it a dour appearance; even the bright red priest's door doesn't help. Inside the church there is not much of interest. The font is a plain octagonal affair devoid of any decoration. The pulpit is Stuart in date but is only notable for its poor quality. The only saving grace is the lovely little 14th c. double-drain piscina with its fine tracery.

FORNHAM

Dedication:	All Saints	
No of Bells:	4	
Deanery 1836:	Thingoe	
Hundred:	Thingoe	
Union house:	Bury St Edmunds	
Deanery 2000:	Thingoe	

2 miles NW of Bury St Edmunds: between Bury St Edmunds & Lackford; in the very centre of the village on the B1106.

O.S. grid ref: TL 837676

Post Code: IP28 6JT

This is a Norman church but only minute parts of it remain: the south doorway, for example, but even this has been much restored over the centuries. The tower has four weighty crocketted pinnacles pointing skyward above the embattled parapet. The pinnacled porch protecting a 15th c. door, and the crenellated south aisle are both 16th c. additions, the latter having some interesting contents. On the north side the transept contains a number of memorial brasses, one to Thomas Barwick, dating back to 1599. Probably the most unusual feature of the church is the position of the 14th c. piscina. Instead of being east of the dropped-sill sedilia, it has been placed, for some unknown reason, to the west. The red-tiled roof reflects quite accurately the character of the interior.

71

FORNHAM

Dedication:	St Genevieve	
No of Bells:	3 in 1553	
Deanery 1836:	Thedwastre	
Hundred:	Thedwastre	
Union house:	Bury St Edmunds	
Deanery 2000:	Thingoe	

3 miles NW of Bury St Edmunds ¾ N of the village between Bury St Edmunds & Culford; from the B1106, south to Fornham Park.
O.S. grid ref: TL 840683
Post Code: IP28 6TT

Standing forlornly in the grounds of Fornham Park, in sight of a nearby cement works, this lovely tower stands as an obelisk to that which was once great. It has been restored and repaired, so someone apart from me is appreciative of its stark beauty. It was in June of 1782 that a fire almost destroyed the church. The parishioners had to travel to Fornham All Saints (see page 71) to worship. It was apparent that the church was not a viable proposition for repair and the nave and chancel walls were removed in 1813. This was a period of great change for the Church and it was left as a monument and ornament within the park. The site was further cleared by the owners in the 1980's and headstones and tombs removed from the site. I do hope that the owners continue to allow us to share it with them.

FORNHAM

Dedication:	St Martin
No of Bells:	6
Deanery 1836:	Thedwastre
Hundred:	Thedwastre
Union house:	Bury St Edmunds
Deanery 2000:	Thingoe

1½ miles N of Bury St Edmunds: between Bury St Edmunds & Culford on the B 1106 (The Street) near The Woolpack PH.

O.S. grid ref: TL 852669

Post Code: IP31 1SW

Standing close to the road, this drab-looking church, looks better on a sunny day. Even the roof of the Victorian south aisle has moss growing on it. Does the sun ever shine here? The north porch is Tudor and is typically of red brick. In the face of the right buttress is a stoup. Inside the church you must be sure to see the finely carved misericorde panels, now part of the lectern and reading desk. They depict the martyrdom of Thomas Beckett on one, and on the other St. Martin of Tours dividing his cloak. It is from St Martin of Tours that the church takes its dedication. The font is disappointingly plain but unusual nevertheless. The altar rails are also plain and of the Stuart period. High on the wall hang the Royal Arms of George III. The kneelers that are scattered throughout the church add some colour.

FRECKENHAM

Dedication:	St Andrew
No of Bells:	5
Deanery 1836:	Fordham
Hundred:	Lackford
Union house:	Mildenhall
Deanery 2000:	Mildenhall

3 miles SW of Mildenhall between Fordham & Worlington: from the B1102 'The Street' turn east at the Golden Boar PH. O.S. grid ref: TL 665717 Post Code: IP28 8JF

Freckenham was at one time a peculiar of the Bishop of Rochester. The nave and chancel were thatched until relatively recently when the roof was tiled. It still retains its steep pitch and strangely has red tiles on the south and grey on the north. The church has been restored and not much of the original remains. A few benches with carved poppy-heads and figures on the ends are interesting and different. In the chancel is a 13th c. piscina with a double drain. Set into the wall of the north aisle is an old alabaster panel, probably an early reredos, uncovered by builders in 1776. It illustrates St Eligius or Eloy (the Patron Saint of blacksmiths) shoeing a horse in his own inimitable way. There is a dormer window in the nave, originally meant to cast light onto the rood, which has since been removed.

GAZELEY

Dedication:	All Saints
No of Bells:	6
Deanery 1836:	Clare
Hundred:	Risbridge
Union house:	Exning
Deanery 2000:	Mildenhall

5 miles E of Newmarket between Kentford & Dalham, close to the three-cross-ways in the centre of Gazeley.

O.S. grid ref: TL 719641

Post Code: CB8 8RB

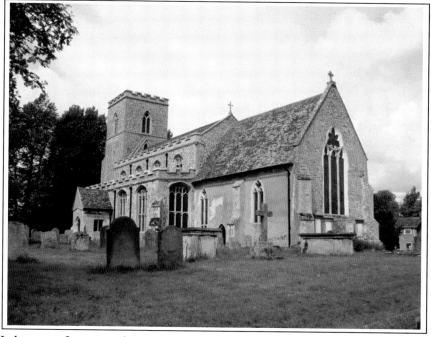

I do not often mention windows, they are too specialised; but here I must point out the unusual. The three-light window at the east end has no arch containing the tracery at the top. It is contained within the cusped head instead. I haven't noticed another like it anywhere. Unlike Freckenham the pitch of the 16th c. nave roof was lessened when the clerestory was added and the roof was tiled. This is clearly noticeable from the marks on the tower. The 14th c. font has traceried panels on the bowl and this is repeated on the shaft.   The piscina in the chancel is contemporary with the font and has a double arch, beside which is a two-height sedilia with, unusually, a carved armrest. Some benches are 15th c., one with pierced lettering. There is some early 16th c. tracery on the pulpit.

GEDDING

Dedication:	St Mary	
No of Bells:	2	
Deanery 1836:	Thedwastre	
Hundred:	Thedwastre	
Union house:	Onehouse	
Deanery 2000:	Lavenham	

6 miles W of Stowmarket between Rattlesden & Bradfield St Clare at the eastern end of Gedding street.

O.S. grid ref: TL 951581

Post Code: IP30 0QD

The tower, or lack of it, is the first thing you will notice. It was capped at the end of the 19th c. when it became unsafe. Around the base it still bears the Chamberlin Arms on the buttress. The age of the structure can be ascertained by the Norman slit windows in the nave walls, one of which has chevron mouldings. There are a number of peculiarities to look for. One is the two recesses under the window sill. It has been suggested that these were reliquaries which were once concealed behind a nave altar. There are squints in the chancel arches. The font is 15th c. and not particularly interesting, but on its pedestal stands the octagonal bowl of what may have been a pillar-stoup. The old rustic benches are my favourite. If you find the church locked, it is worth the effort to obtain the key.

GIPPING

Dedication:	St Nicholas
No of Bells:	1
Deanery 1836:	Stow
Hundred:	Stow
Union house:	Onehouse
Deanery 2000:	Stowmarket

4 miles NE of Stowmarket
between Old Newton &
Mendlesham, near
Pleasantview Cottages head
towards Chapel Farm.
O.S. grid ref: TM 072635
Post Code: IP14 4PT

It may not be obvious at first, but the churchyard is completely bereft of headstones or monuments of any kind. The reason for this is that it was originally a private chapel, built by Sir James Tyrell, infamous for the murder of the young princes in the White Tower in 1483. Above the door of the vestry is the inscription 'Pray for Sir Jamys Tirrell ...'. The upper part of the tower has been rebuilt, but the black and white flint chequer-work is remarkable, and the detail in the stonework is well worth a closer look. Inside the church the east end is beautifully painted with drapes around columns, looking as real as the rest of the church. The north door is still barred against those who wish the occupants harm. The font is circular on an octagonal base and shaft. The benches at the west end are plain and grey with age.

GISLINGHAM

Dedication:	St Mary	
No of Bells:	6	
Deanery 1836:	Hartismere	
Hundred:	Hartismere	
Union house:	Eye & Wortham	
Deanery 2000:	Hartismere	

5 miles SW of Eye
between Thornham Magna
& Walsham le Willows, at
the junction of Mellis Road
& Thornham Road.
O.S. grid ref: TM 076717
Post Code: IP23 8HP

From the outside the outstanding feature of this church is its red brick tower. It was built in 1639 after the original fell forty years earlier. There are two scratch dials to look out for. The entrance is through the late 15th c. north porch built by Robert Chapman. Above the nave is a lovely example of a double hammerbeam roof. It has an arch-braced battlemented collar. The double-decker pulpit, complete with back and canopy, is reached by 8 steps and encircled by an 18th c. box pew. Part of the old screen remains and illustrates the skill of the wood-carver. In the chancel is a marble and painted stone monument to Anthony Bedingfield showing him in academic robes. The font is a typical East Anglian type, somewhat less common in the west of the county than in the east.

GLEMSFORD

Dedication:	St Mary	
No of Bells:	6	
Deanery 1836:	Sudbury	
Hundred:	Babergh	
Union house:	Sudbury	
Deanery 2000:	Sudbury	

5 miles NW of Sudbury between Cavendish & Boxted, on the B1065 in Churchgate (Street).

O.S. grid ref: TL 834483

Post Code: CO10 7QE

This grand church started life in the 13th c. but what you see today is almost all of the 15th. The porch has some fine flint panelling and flushwork. Around the south aisle and porch is a parapet of early 16th c. date. The Jacobean pulpit has carvings of grapes and on the brackets some strange representations of birds. The octagonal 15th c. font is carved with figures of the Virgin, a bishop, and two evangelistic emblems. Two panels were mutilated by Dowsing's men. The shaft is traceried and angels support the bowl. George Cavendish is buried here. He was Cardinal Wolsey's servant and he retired here after Wolsey's death. For some reason the pews and benches have been ripped out and horrible cheap wooden chairs installed in their place.

GREAT ASHFIELD

Dedication:	All Saints
No of Bells:	5
Deanery 1836:	Blackbourn
Hundred:	Blackbourn
Union house:	Onehouse
Deanery 2000:	Ixworth

7 miles NW of Stowmarket between Badwell Ash & Elmswell, at the northern end of Elmswell Road, in the village street.
O.S. grid ref: TL 995677
Post Code: IP31 3HE

Above the plain parapet on the top of the tower is a distinguishing spirelet. The porch is built of 16th c. Tudor red brick and has flint flushwork panels and crow-step gable. Some early 13th c. wall remains between the pillars of the north aisle arcade. The nave roof is a simple arch-braced type. The finely carved pulpit is unusually square, standing on cushion feet with the original back and sounding board, dated 1619. The holy table bears the same date, and the same style is also reflected in the reredos. There are some interesting bench-end carvings to look out for. The octagonal font is plain and undecorated. The old parish chest is a good example of its kind and is iron-bound. The church also possesses an iron-bound chalice case, but this is kept elsewhere.

GREAT BARTON

Dedication:	Holy Innocents
No of Bells:	5
Deanery 1836:	Thedwastre
Hundred:	Thedwastre
Union house:	Bury St Edmunds
Deanery 2000:	Thingoe

2 miles NE of Bury St
Edmunds between Bury St
Edmunds & Pakenham, off
the A143, ½ S of the
village, signposted.
O.S. grid ref: TL 890660
Post Code: IP31 2QS

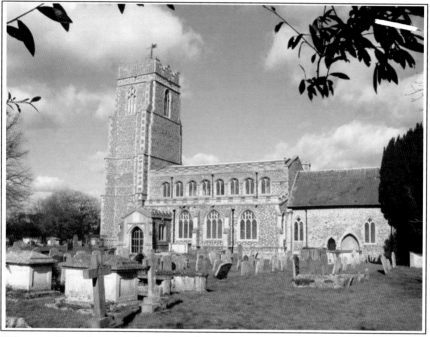

What a fine impressive church this is. The tower dominates the churchyard, sitting a good half-mile south of the village it serves. It is unfortunate that the south porch is cement-rendered: its only saving grace is the fine embattled gable. In the outer south wall of the nave is an arched and recessed tomb, its occupant unknown. The chancel is the oldest part of the church, being 13th c.. The clerestory, which supports a single hammerbeam roof, admits plenty of light into the nave even on a dull day. Inside the church the small octagonal 13th c. font has four detached columns and a central shaft and is overshadowed by its tall carved cover. Many of the bench-ends and poppy-heads are copies, but some are original. There is a monument to Sir Henry Bunbury (1860) in the north chancel wall.

GREAT BRADLEY

Dedication:	St Mary
No of Bells:	3
Deanery 1836:	Clare
Hundred:	Rissbridge
Union house:	Haverhill
Deanery 2000:	Clare

6 miles N of Haverhill between Little Thurlow & Brinkley, Cambs. Turn off the B1061 opposite The Fox PH and follow road 400 yds.
O.S. grid ref: TL 674531
Post Code: CB8 9LT

At first glance this charming little Norman church seems nothing out of the ordinary, but it houses one of the earliest bells in the county. Dating from the early 1300's it is inscribed, 'RICARD DE WYMBIS ME FACIT'. Although the tower has been cement-rendered this is probably the best example of how it should be done. The decorated Norman doorway, with two engaged columns, is protected by an elaborate Tudor red-brick porch which has eight empty niches and a lofty crow-stepped gable. The nave has a wagon roof with tie-beams and king posts. The piscina is 14th c., the octagonal font a century later. The pulpit is 18th c. and retains its back and sounding board. Behind the pulpit is a small recess and there is another on the opposite wall; each contain a small Norman piscina.

GREAT CORNARD

Dedication:	St Andrew
No of Bells:	5
Deanery 1836:	Sudbury
Hundred:	Babergh
Union house:	Sudbury
Deanery 2000:	Sudbury

1 mile SE of Sudbury
between Sudbury & Bures
on the B1508. Unmissable.
Best to park in Church
Road, off the main road.
O.S. grid ref: TL 883404
Post Code: CO10 0EL

A beautifully proportioned shingle-clad broached spire surmounts the 14th c. tower. On the north side a brick stair turret has been added to allow easy access to the clock mechanism. The structure is basically 14th century but was heavily restored during the Victorian spending spree. Further 20th c. 'restoration'(?) has obliterated some wall paintings of the Elizabethan period that were on the wall of the north aisle. The font bowl has some armorial shields around its perimeter but is nothing special. Someone has hoicked several lovely cast iron monuments from the graves and leaned them against the wall of the churchyard, making them an easy target for metal thieves. I hope they are haunted by those who paid for them originally. Very disappointing after a promising start.

GREAT FINBOROUGH

Dedication:	St Andrew
No of Bells:	6
Deanery 1836:	Stow
Hundred:	Stow
Union house:	Onehouse
Deanery 2000:	Stowmarket

2½ miles W of Stowmarket between Stowmarket & Buxhall, just off the B1115. Centre of the village, in Church Road.
O.S. grid ref: TM 013579
Post Code: IP14 3AD

This is the third church to occupy this site. Built between 1874 and 1877 and largely financed by Robert Pettiward, this Victorian church is recognisable anywhere. The spire was an afterthought added in memory of Pettiward's wife. It has a square base and flying buttresses supporting the central octagonal belfry stage. Built of traditional flint and stone, entry is through the south porch. Inside the church, there is open space, no side aisles. The font piscina and sedilia are all contemporary with the building. The rood screen is a memorial to those who fell in the Great War whilst other memorials in the side chapel are to the Pettiward and Woolaston families. The finest, depicting the good Samaritan, is to Roger Pettiward (1833). Many of the monuments are originally from the old church.

GREAT LIVERMERE

Dedication:	St Peter
No of Bells:	5
Deanery 1836:	Thedwastre
Hundred:	Thedwastre
Union house:	Bury St Edmunds
Deanery 2000:	Ixworth

5 miles N of Bury St Edmunds, between Ampton & Troston. At Gt. Barton take Brand Lane to Livermere, turn left at the Post Office.
O.S. grid ref: TL 885713
Post Code: IP31 1JR

The nave is still thatched although the 700 year old chancel has been tiled for some time. What is left of the tower is 13th c. and is capped by a wooden belfry stage which is covered in grey tiles. The body of the church is cement-rendered but this has been competently done and doesn't look at all out of place. The crenulated porch is 15th c. The octagonal font is 100 years earlier and decorated with traceried patterns on the bowl and a plain shaft. In the walls there are unusual niches; the reason for their presence is unknown. The rood beam at one time rested on the two carved corbels just above the springing of the chancel arch. The paintings are in very poor condition now but at one time must have decorated the whole interior of this lovely little church. The interior could do with a coat of paint here and there.

GREAT SAXHAM

Dedication:	St Andrew
No of Bells:	3
Deanery 1836:	Thingoe
Hundred:	Thingoe
Union house:	Bury St Edmunds
Deanery 2000:	Thingoe

4 miles W of Bury St Edmunds between Little Saxham & Hargrave, on the street as it passes through the village; nr The Hall.
O.S. grid ref: TL 788628
Post Code: IP29 5JW

This is not an ancient church although it retains its two Norman doorways. It was for the most part rebuilt in 1708 after the Norman church started to crumble. It is so nice to find a church that can be viewed from almost any angle without trees blocking the view. Inside the church the 15th c. octagonal font has a simple traceried bowl. The pulpit is from the Stuart period and has carved arcaded panels. More carvings are to be found on the bench ends, some of which are older than others. The pelican in piety features more than once on the stalls in the chancel. On the wall of the chancel the merchant John Eldred, who died in 1632 and who introduced nutmeg to England, looks down, closely resembling Sir Francis Drake. The Royal Arms of Queen Anne dated 1702 hang on the nave wall.

GREAT THURLOW

Dedication:	All Saints
No of Bells:	5
Deanery 1836:	Clare
Hundred:	Risbridge
Union house:	Haverhill
Deanery 2000:	Clare

4 miles N of Haverhill
between Great Wratting &
Great Bradley Turn off the
B1061 at the War Memorial
into Bury Road.
O.S. grid ref: TL 680503
Post Code: CB9 7LF

Easily recognisable by the elaborate bell cage sitting atop the tower.
The chancel too is considerably smaller than the nave in height.
Before entering the church take a look at the quoins at the east end of
the chancel. They are carved to create engaged shafts, not unique but
uncommon. The porch is on the north due to the proximity of the
road. The 12th c. font is the treasure here and although it is not over-
elaborate it does have nice arcaded sides to the bowl. The pulpit is of
the Stuart period and also bears some carving. The south aisle
contains two cornices which appear to be from an old screen, the
lower part of which is in the chancel. An early brass depicting a man
in armour, and his wife, is dated 1460. Another, 70 years later, is of
Thomas Underhill and Anne his wife.

GREAT WALDINGFIELD

Dedication: St Lawrence
No of Bells: 6
Deanery 1836: Sudbury
Hundred: Babergh
Union house: Sudbury
Deanery 2000: Sudbury

3 miles NE of Sudbury between Sudbury & Little Waldingfield. Turn off the B1115 at Babergh Hall Farm and follow road east. O.S. grid ref: TL 912439
Post Code: CO10 0TJ

Unmissable, and standing right beside the road, is this very fine, elegant looking church. The clerestory, porch and tower are all embattled. Above the four clerestory windows is an inscription asking for prayers for the builder. There are two stair turrets, one to the top of the tower and the other to the parapet above the south aisle. The real treasures lie inside the church. The 15th c. font is possibly re-cut from a much earlier bowl. The font cover tries to imitate that of Ufford, but fails in height and detail. There is a chair and corner table to demonstrate the carver's skill. The walls of the chancel sanctuary are lined with panels of marble fragments, supposedly collected 'from the ruins of the heathen temples of Rome in 1867'. The Royal Arms are of George III.

GREAT WELNETHAM

Dedication: St Thomas Becket
No of Bells: 1
Deanery 1836: Thedwastre
Hundred: Thedwastre
Union house: Bury St Edmunds
Deanery 2000: Lavenham

4 miles S of Bury St Edmunds between Bury & Bradfield Combust, off the A134 into Stanningfield Rd, by the primary school.
O.S. grid ref: TL 878593
Post Code: IP30 0TY

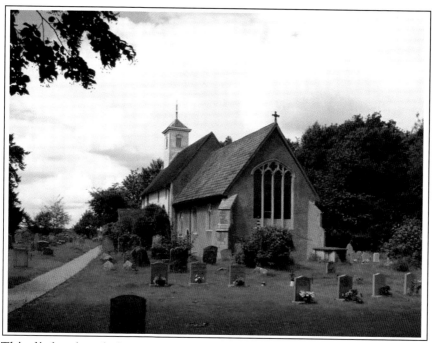

This little church has no tower, but instead a small wooden belfry which was erected in 1749 and paid for by one James Merest. At the junction of the nave and chancel there is a small carving in a quoin of a snake. Inside the church everything seems a little clinical. The 15th c. font is octagonal with a simple quatrefoil design. The piscina in the nave has a double drain hole and a cusped arch above. The three-seat sedilia, separated by pillars, has barely enough headroom to be practical. Linking the nave and chancel are wall tiles bearing religious emblems which were placed there in 1911. They offend my eye: regrettably they clash horribly with the floor tiles. Above is a memorial to Charles Batterley (1722) and his wife Elizabeth. Another, bearing skull and crossbones is to Richard Gipps (1660)

GREAT WRATTING
Dedication: St Mary
No of Bells: 1
Deanery 1836:   Clare
Hundred: Risbridge
Union house: Haverhill
Deanery 2000:   Clare

2 miles NE of Haverhill
between Haverhill & Great
Thurlow. Turn off the A143
at the factory X roads and
follow for ½ mile.
O.S. grid ref: TL 688482
Post Code: CB9 7HD

Here is a church with some unusually elaborate head and footstones in the churchyard. The church itself has been restored but most of its lower portions are original. The roof retains its original pitch, but the line of the thatched roof can be clearly seen on the east face of the tower. The piscina is a good example, still retaining its stone credence shelf. The sedilia are of the same date but have been modified with wooden panels set into the backs and wooden seats. The internal chancel walls are original 13th c. and have two aumbries built into them. The parish chest is late 17th c. The font is the most unusual thing this church had to offer with its 36-inch external diameter bowl looked enormous. These days a modern wooden font with a stainless steel bowl is used instead.

GROTON

Dedication:	St Bartholomew	
No of Bells:	5	
Deanery 1836:	Sudbury	
Hundred:	Babergh	
Union house:	Sudbury	
Deanery 2000:	Sudbury	

6 miles E of Sudbury
between Boxford &
Edwardstone, hard to miss
on Church Street near the
Fox and Hounds PH.
O.S. grid ref: TL 959416
Post Code: CO10 5ED

Just inside the porch is a notice pointing out that Groton is the proud possessor of the oldest headstone in the county. Most of the church dates from around the end of the 15th c., but the roof of the nave is 200 years later. This was probably when the clerestory was added. Parts of the church, especially the lower part of the tower, are 13th c. The octagonal font is rather uninspiring and plain, but was attractively planted as an indoor garden when I visited. The interior is painted pink which I found strange, although quite pleasing. John Winthrop sailed to America in 1629 and became first Governor of Massachusetts and founder of Boston. He was born here in 1588 and died in 1649. The glass in the windows serve as a memorial to many other members of the Winthrop family.

91

HADLEIGH *****
Dedication: St Mary
No of Bells: 8 + 1 clock bell
Deanery 1836: Bocking, Essex
Hundred: Cosford
Union house: Semer
Deanery 2000: Hadleigh

9 miles W of Ipswich
between Ipswich &
Boxford, just off Hadleigh
High Street in Church
Street. Parking not easy.
O.S. grid ref: TM O25424
Post Code: IP7 5DU

This is an old church despite its appearance. Obviously restoration has taken place over the years, but has been well executed. Even the clock bell which hangs on the east face of the leaded spire is 13th c. and possibly the oldest bell in the county. The spire is a little later. The south porch which is early 15th c. was reduced in height and the chamber above removed many years ago. Inside the porch the door bears some old tracery. The fine octagonal font is 15th c. and is decorated with 16 panels. Suspended above the font is the splendid cover. The pulpit is supported on a pillared stone base. The piscina and sedilia are replicas. North of the sanctuary is an Easter sepulchre recess with panelled vaulting and which adjoins a 15th c. vestry. The official guide book will tell you much more than I can include here.

HARGRAVE

Dedication:	St Edmund		6 miles WSW of Bury St Edmunds between Ousden & Chevington, north of the village centre in the grounds of Hargrave Hall.
No of Bells:	3		
Deanery 1836:	Thingoe		
Hundred:	Thingoe		
Union house:	Bury St Edmunds		O.S. grid ref: TL 766608
Deanery 2000:	Thingoe		Post Code: IP29 5HH

The tower is a Tudor red-brick construction with a plain parapet and a stair turret on the SE corner. There is a Norman doorway which before WWII was protected by a porch until it was destroyed by a stray German bomb. Just inside the door there is a stoup and in the nave stands a rusty old tortoise stove. The font is 15th c. with simple quatrefoil decoration on each of the eight facets of the bowl. The cover is a simple octagonal skeletal dome. The screen is well but crudely carved, especially the upper part, probably by a local artisan. At one time it was even more elaborate, but has suffered the ravages of time and is now damaged. Originally it had a canopy, but this too has gone. In the chancel a 13th c. piscina with its double arch is adjacent to the dropped-sill sedilia.

HARLESTON

		2½ miles NW of
Dedication:	St Augustine	Stowmarket between
No of Bells:	1	Onehouse & Shelland. Take
Deanery 1836:	Stow	the Haughley Road from
Hundred:	Stow	Shelland, nr Harleston Hall.
Union house:	Onehouse	O.S. grid ref: TM 018603
Deanery 2000:	Stowmarket	Post Code: IP14 3JQ

This is the image of what most small Norman parish churches must have looked like when they were first built. Thatched and towerless with, perhaps, a bellcote atop the apex of the roof. The windows however would have been much smaller or even non-existent. The plain Norman doorway is shielded by a pair of Irish yew trees growing far too close to the wall. It wouldn't surprise me to find the nave floor being pushed upwards by the roots next time I visit. On the north wall another Norman door has been filled in. Inside the nave the screen is 14th c. and is typical of the period. Most of the remaining interior features are Victorian, including the lovely carved angels, looking for all the world like fairies. The font is a simple octagonal bowl and shaft sitting on a square base.

HARTEST		7½ miles N of Sudbury
Dedication:	All Saints	between Boxted &
No of Bells:	5	Lawshall. From the B1066
Deanery 1836:	Sudbury	turn east at the War
Hundred:	Babergh	Memorial on the Green.
Union house:	Sudbury	O.S. grid ref: TL 834523
Deanery 2000:	Sudbury	Post Code: IP29 4DH

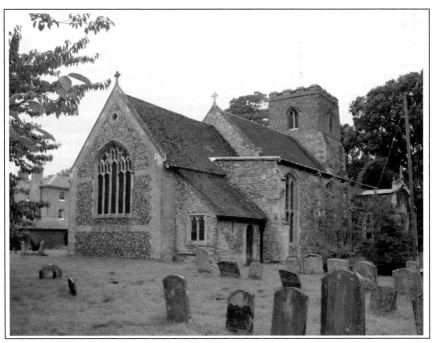

A hotch-potch of add-ons gives this church a certain character, love it or hate it. The pitch of every roof is different from its neighbour, Tudor brickwork repairs intrude in the flint walls, but look up at the tower and you can't help but admire the fine brickwork below the crenellations. There are porches north and south, the latter having a stoup within. The building is mostly 15th c. having been heavily restored about that time. The piscina is in a pillar which was, I think, at one time part of the nave wall before the north aisle was built. The octagonal pulpit is Stuart and has simple decorated panels on each face. Apart from the splendid carving on the roof beams, I found little of interest inside the church, and returned outside where I spent ages examining the exterior of the building and the graveyard.

HAUGHLEY

Dedication:	St Mary
No of Bells:	5
Deanery 1836:	Stow
Hundred:	Stow
Union house:	Onehouse
Deanery 2000:	Stowmarket

3 miles NW of Stowmarket between Wetherden & Old Newton. Once in Haughley find it in Duke Street near the King's Arms.

O.S. grid ref: TM 026623
Post Code: IP14 3QS

The southern tower looks totally misplaced and detached from the church but it is the main entrance, now joined to the church by the south aisle. It is an unusual configuration. Above the roofline of the nave, a sanctus bell is hung in a small stone turret. At one time fire buckets hung from the ceiling of the porch, but now only their hooks remain. Inside the nave now however, four remaining buckets inaccessibly hang from a rail. The south doorway is late 13th c. and is of a fine quality with two engaged columns either side. The 15th c. font is a well-carved traditional East Anglian type with wodewoses and lions around the base. The nave roof has large floral bosses at the intersections of the timbers while angels with outspread wings hang from the timber corbels.

HAVERHILL

Dedication:	St Mary
No of Bells:	5
Deanery 1836:	Clare
Hundred:	Risbridge
Union house:	Haverhill
Deanery 2000:	Clare

12 miles S of Newmarket between Great Wratting & Helions Bumpstead, Essex. The church is in the town centre near the shops.
O.S. grid ref: TL 671455
Post Code: CB9 8AA

Haverhill's splendid and richly endowed church suffered a serious fire in 1665 and very little remained except the 14th c. nave walls and tower. The three pinnacles are carved grotesque figures. At the fourth corner is the stair turret, which continues above the embattled parapet. What we see today is a typical town church built about the same time as St Paul's Cathedral. The font is the original from before the fire. The font cover is the work of Frederick Gibberd, famed for being the designer of Liverpool's great Catholic Cathedral. Unfortunately, the church is usually kept locked. There is little else of historical or architectural interest to see here. The interest lies in the rise of Haverhill as a town, and its trials and tribulations through the centuries, to become Suffolk's fifth largest town today.

HAWKEDON

Dedication:	St Mary
No of Bells:	5
Deanery 1836:	Clare
Hundred:	Risbridge
Union house:	Sudbury
Deanery 2000:	Clare

8 miles SW of Bury St Edmunds between Boxted & Denston in the centre of the village near Hawkedon Hall.

O.S. grid ref: TL 797529

Post Code: IP29 4NN

This is the site that greets you when entering this lovely little village. The early 15th c. church sits right in the middle of the green within its walled churchyard. The south porch has stoups outside and in. The roof of the nave has arch-braced tie-beams and is plastered between the single framed rafters. The font is Norman and was originally square, but two corners have been removed to allow it to sit into a corner. Recycling had its place here too, when in 1750 the Royal Arms of Charles II were modified to those of George II. The holy table and pulpit are early Stuart, but the bench-ends and poppy-heads are completely unlike any I have seen elsewhere, except perhaps those at Withersfield. The carved grotesques and figures are worthy of close examination.

HAWSTEAD ****

Dedication:	All Saints
No of Bells:	3 + sanctus bell
Deanery 1836:	Thingoe
Hundred:	Thingoe
Union house:	Bury St Edmunds
Deanery 2000:	Thingoe

3 miles S of Bury St
Edmunds between
Sicklesmere & Whepstead
turn west at the three-cross-
ways off Bury Road.
O.S. grid ref: TL 855592
Post Code: IP29 5NT

As I approached this church through the jungle before me, I had no
idea what treats lay in store. The 16th c. tower has various crests and
motifs in the flushwork of the parapet. Inside the south porch a
Norman doorway with a chevroned arch greets you, and there is
another in the north wall. The roof of the nave is of single
hammerbeam construction. The font is square, sitting on a central
octagonal shaft, with a pillar at each corner, and a relatively modern
lid. The iron-bound chest is 14th c., the wooden lectern 15th. The
pulpit is 16th c. but it has been restored. It is in the chancel where I
encountered some of the finest memorials I have seen in a small
parish church. They are mostly of the Drury, Metcalf and Cullum
families and above them is a ceiling that is a treat to behold.

HENGRAVE

Dedication:	St John the Lateran
No of Bells:	1
Deanery 1836:	Thingoe
Hundred:	Thingoe
Union house:	Bury St Edmunds
Deanery 2000:	Thingoe

3 miles NW of Bury St Edmunds between Bury St Edmunds & Lackford Only accessible by permission from Hengrave Hall.
O.S. grid ref: TL 824685
Post Code: IP28 6LS

This church has not been the parish church for many years. It belongs to the Hall in whose grounds it sits. It is only accessible by permission from the owner. The tower is remarkable in that it is very probably Saxon. It has an internal diameter of 12 feet 9 inches, and tapers slightly inwards. Inside the porch we see an elaborate stoup and find that the church was rebuilt by Sir Thomas Hemegrave (1419). Much of what remains in the church is from that period; certainly the font is, which according to H. Munro Cautley stands on the upturned bowl of another. The monuments are quite outstanding: that of Margaret, Countess of Bath and her three husbands, John Bourchier, Thomas Kitson and Sir Richard Longe, and yet another of Sir Thomas Kitson lying between his two wives.

HEPWORTH

Dedication: St Peter
No of Bells: 5
Deanery 1836:   Blackbourn
Hundred: Blackbourn
Union house: Thetford
Deanery 2000:   Ixworth

10   miles WSW of Diss
between   Wattisfield &
Stanton turn off the A143
into Hepworth Street then
into Church Lane.
O.S. grid ref: TL 987748
Post Code: IP22 2QE

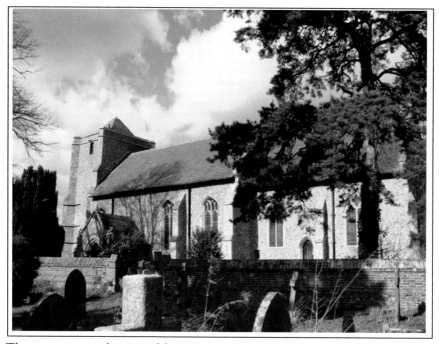

The tower was shortened in 1677 and given a tiled pyramidal cap and dormer widow. The church suffered a fire in 1898 when some of the original material and the thatched roof lost. A 19th c. iron strapping wraps itself around the buttresses holding the structure together; this is an ongoing problem even though the tower was shortened. The font is modern and plain but the cover is intricate to the extreme: alas, it is not what it used to be, clumsy restoration having marred its detail, but its charm and attraction remain. At 12½ feet tall it is $^2/_3$ as tall as the one at Ufford (E. Sfk. p. 266). Some benches were rescued from the fire and are simple in their workmanship. A set of hand-bells donated to the church in 1920 hang in the tower arch. The church is always kept locked, but the Rector's address is posted.

HERRINGSWELL

Dedication: St Ethelbert
No of Bells: 3
Deanery 1836:   Fordham
Hundred: Lackford
Union house: Mildenhall
Deanery 2000:   Mildenhall

1½ miles E of Red Lodge
between   Red Lodge &
Tuddenham, best accessed
from the cross-roads north
of Tuddenham.
O.S. grid ref: TL 718700
Post Code: IP28 6ST

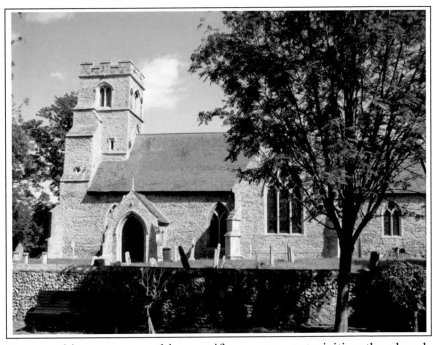

You would never come this way if you were not visiting the church. It is well off the beaten track. Just inside the gate there is a rather impressive sculpted monument to Herbert Davis (1899). The tower is unusual in that the buttresses are also utilised as stair turrets to the upper stages. The east wall of the tower is supported on columns, arches and flying buttresses internally, easily visible at the west end of the nave. The tower is older by far than the main body of the church as the original was burned down in 1869, but some of the early Norman walls remain: the engaged columns at the eastern corners of what was the chancel, now the nave, for example. The furnishings are attractive but of no real age or interest to the architect or historian.

HESSETT

		5 miles SE of Bury St
Dedication:	St Ethelbert	Edmunds between Beyton
No of Bells:	5	& Gedding almost opposite
Deanery 1836:	Thedwastre	the Five Bells PH in Hessett
Hundred:	Thedwastre	Street.
Union house:	Onehouse	O.S. grid ref: TL 936618
Deanery 2000:	Lavenham	Post Code: IP30 9AX

Here is an interesting little church. In the churchyard you will find
the base of a 15th c. cross and part of the upright, still in the original
position. A rarity indeed. The tower is beautifully proportioned and
is decorated from its pierced parapet to the chequer-work around the
base. The fine 15th c. clerestory and the porch also have pierced
parapets and it all fits together magnificently. An inscription tells the
viewer more. Inside the church more treats await the visitor. Within
the porch is the base of a stoup, the late 14th c. font is carved from
top to bottom and sits on an octagonal base with an inscription. The
15th c. screen has been repainted, and the wall paintings carefully
preserved. The seven deadly sins are represented in the form of a
tree. The iron-bound chest is huge. Charles II's Arms hang above it.

HIGHAM GREEN

Dedication:	St Stephen	
No of Bells:	1	
Deanery 1836:	Clare	
Hundred:	Lackford	
Union house:	Mildenhall	
Deanery 2000:	Thingoe	

6 miles W of Bury St Edmunds between Kentford & Barrow, off the A14 west of Bury near Lodge Farm.

O.S. grid ref: TL 746655
Post Code: IP28 6NH

This is a Victorian church which was built from scratch in 1861 at a cost of £3,600. It is built in the traditional English style, designed by Sir George Gilbert Scott, from flint and stone. It has a round tower, which includes a belfry stage with blind arcading, and is topped by a conical cap which some seem to regard as a spire. The stumpy font sits in a baptistery beneath the arches of the tower. The font and pulpit are a matching pair, set on pillars of marble, with reliefs of Sts Peter and Paul. Why not Stephen, I ask? It is he to whom the church is dedicated. Although they have been out of use for hundreds of years, a two-seat sedilia has been included in the design for the sake of authenticity. There is however no piscina. It is a pity all Victorian churches do not suit their surroundings as well as this.

HINDERCLAY

Dedication:	St Mary
No of Bells:	6
Deanery 1836:	Blackbourn
Hundred:	Blackbourn
Union house:	Thetford
Deanery 2000:	Ixworth

8 miles NW of Eye
between Rickinghall &
Thelnetham. From
Rickinghall Inferior or
Bottesdale follow signposts
O.S. grid ref: TM 027768
Post Code: IP22 1HN

Shrouded by trees in the summer, this is a delightful church, seemingly dwarfed by its tower, until you realise that what you thought was the nave is actually the south aisle; but it is not a recent addition, the porch attached to it is 14th c. and still retains its original timber arch. The north door is the older of the two, being late 12th c. A scratch dial is there to be found. Inside the church the arches of the 13th c. pier arcade, which forms the division between the nave and south aisle, spring from only five feet above floor level. This does not account however for the dropped window sill sedilia being only a few inches from the floor. The chancel floor has been raised at some time in the past, in common with many others. The 14th c. arched and cusped piscina opens into the window reveal.

HITCHAM

Dedication:	All Saints
No of Bells:	6
Deanery 1836:	Sudbury
Hundred:	Cosford
Union house:	Semer
Deanery 2000:	Lavenham

6 miles NW of Hadleigh between Brettenham & Bildeston, on the B1115, just south of The Street in the village.

O.S. grid ref: TL 984511

Post Code: IP7 7NN

The tower here has eight buttresses, two at each corner, as at Monks Eleigh. There is also a stair turret on the south side leading to the belfry. Inside, the eastern buttresses overlap the west arches of the nave, indicating that the tower once stood independent of the 14th c. church. The porch has some attractive panelled flushwork and the four-light clerestory and south aisle have embattled parapets to match. The 17th c. roof of the nave is a double hammerbeam and carries the Arms of James I at one end and those of Charles I at the other. The roof in the chancel has an unusual sort of barrel ceiling. There is an interesting lower portion of the old 16th c. rood screen, depicting eight angels carrying instruments of the Passion, instead of the usual saints. The font is 19th c and the cover is even more recent.

HONINGTON

Dedication:	All Saints	
No of Bells:	3	
Deanery 1836:	Blackbourn	
Hundred:	Blackbourn	
Union house:	Thetford	
Deanery 2000:	Ixworth	

7 miles SE of Thetford, Norfolk, between Ixworth Thorpe & Fakenham Magna, just off the A1088 east at the crossroads.
O.S. grid ref: TL 913745
Post Code: IP31 1RG

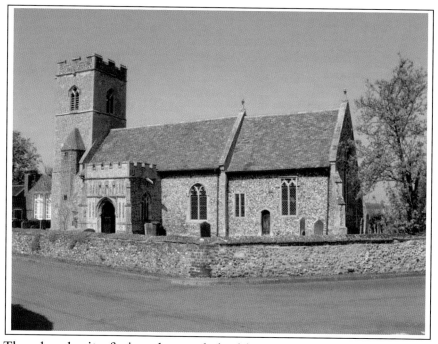

The church sits facing the road, inviting you to enter. On passing through the 15th c. embattled porch and beneath the niches above the doorway you come across the richly carved Norman doorway with four engaged columns, one with knops. The archway has three carved orders and carved dripstones. Above the arch, the keystone is also carved but unrecognisable, possibly a face. The chancel arch is also the Norman-built original. The font is the most impressive item to see here, with fine carvings on the eight facets of the bowl, one depicting the crucifixion. The bench-ends (although of meagre quality) have carvings of a monkey, a woman playing bagpipes and a unicorn scratching his back with his horn. A late 16th c. brass depicts George Duke (1594) in Elizabethan dress.

HOPTON

Dedication: All Saints
No of Bells: 6
Deanery 1836: Blackbourn
Hundred: Blackbourn
Union house: Thetford
Deanery 2000: Ixworth

8 miles W of Eye between Barningham & Garboldisham, directly off the B1111 Bury Road, as it passes through the village.
O.S. grid ref: TL 993790
Post Code: IP22 2QY

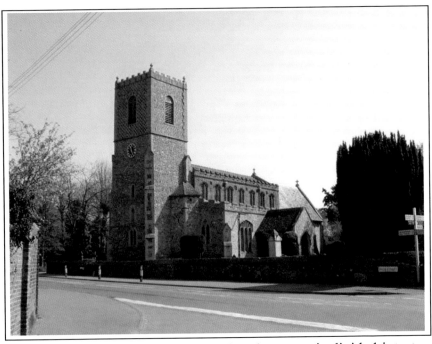

You will probably instantly notice that the tower is divided into two distinct sections. The lower part is 14th c. but the upper, belfry stage, with its fine chequer-work and delicate crenellations, is 18th c. The clerestory which is of red brick is a Tudor addition. Inside the nave there is a hammer beam and arch-braced roof with a very shallow pitch. The hammerbeams are carved into figures with musical instruments, peering down on those looking up. The door to the turret stairs is iron-clad; so too is the huge 14th c. parish chest or trunk, which has obviously been hewn straight from a tree trunk (hence the name). The piscina is very simple and the sedilia is just a straightforward window seat. The Victorian bier is on display and could even still be in use if and when the occasion arises.

HORRINGER

		2 miles SW of Bury St
Dedication:	St Leonard	Edmunds between Bury St
No of Bells:	6	Edmunds & Chedburgh,
Deanery 1836:	Thingoe	beside the A143 at the
Hundred:	Thingoe	entrance to Ickworth Park
Union house:	Bury St Edmunds	O.S. grid ref: TL 825620
Deanery 2000:	Thingoe	Post Code: IP29 5QB

Before the 19th c. known as Horningsheath, a more pleasing name in my opinion. The tower with its croqueted pinnacles was built in the early 14th c. and updated 400 years later in 1703. Standing at the gates of Ickworth Park, the church is often ignored by the day tripper in favour of the romance of Ickworth House. The whole church was over-restored in 1818 by the owners of the Hall and work continued throughout the 19th c. to enhance the eastern entrance. Little of genuine historical interest remains in the church to attract the visitor. Even the mediaeval font has been given the modern treatment with contemporary heraldic shields painted on the bowl. It may be as it once was, but I have become accustomed to the natural appearance of stone. Call me old-fashioned if you like!

HUNDON

Dedication:	All Saints
No of Bells:	6
Deanery 1836:	Clare
Hundred:	Risbridge
Union house:	Haverhill
Deanery 2000:	Clare

5 miles NE of Haverhill between Barnardiston & Clare, in the centre of the village on North Street, near the Post Office.
O.S. grid ref: TL 738487
Post Code: CO10 8ED

In 1914 the church caught fire and the interior was partly destroyed, but the structure of the building remained intact. The 14th c. tower, with its heavy buttresses and stair turret which continues above the parapet is impressive. Atop the stair turret is a bellcote resembling the one at Cavendish (see p. 38). The amply proportioned south porch which has suffered damage over the years has a room above. There are signs of an earlier church and parts of a splendid 13th c. tomb are evidence of this. It is unfortunate that nature, although beautiful, can be destructive, and the ivy growing up the north walls is no exception. The damp it is causing is damaging the fabric of the building. So easy to prevent, so costly to repair. Come on, Hundon, or your new organ will go rusty.

HUNSTON

Dedication:	St Michael	
No of Bells:	3	
Deanery 1836:	Blackbourn	
Hundred:	Blackbourn	
Union house:	Onehouse	
Deanery 2000:	Ixworth	

8 miles NE of Bury St Edmunds between Walsham le Willows & Stowlangtoft. Turn south in the village near Dairy Farm. O.S. grid ref: TL 975680
Post Code: IP31 3EN

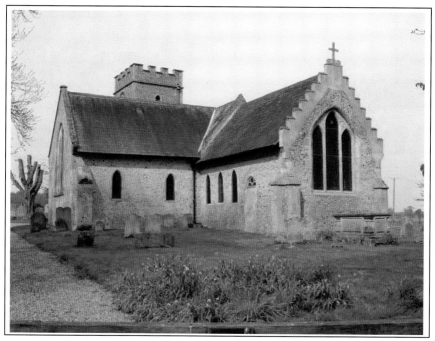

There has been a church here since Norman times, but this isn't as the Normans built it. It has been changed almost beyond recognition, although much of its history is still here to see if you know where to look. The porch has been completely replaced by a modern version. The roof is no longer thatched, but there is a lovely crow-step east gable to the chancel. There are 13th c. windows, some of which are built into the walls of the chancel. A double 13th c. piscina with cusped heads has been incorporated into the south-east angle of the disproportionately large south transept. The church is obviously well cared for and used on a regular basis. It is a pity that it cannot, because of its position, be left open for the occasional visitor. There is however a notice giving the whereabouts of the key.

ICKLINGHAM   *****   4 miles SE of Mildenhall
Dedication: All Saints   between Barton Mills &
No of Bells: 3   Lackford , on the A1101 at
Deanery 1836:   Fordham   the east end of the village,
Hundred: Lackford   just off The Street.
Union house: Mildenhall   O.S. grid ref: TL 775726
Deanery 2000:   Mildenhall   Post Code: IP28 6PL

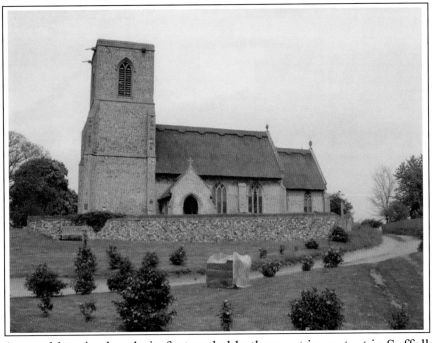

A very historic church, in fact probably the most important in Suffolk
in many respects. It has been cared for by the Churches Conservation
Trust since 1973, some wonderful work has been carried out here.
The church has been out of regular use for well over 100 years and
that, ironically, is what has preserved it. It was not restored by the
Victorians. It is unmissable and has space to park your car. The walls
of the nave are 12th c. Inside you will see what a mediaeval church
used to look like after the Reformation. The unique octagonal font is
early 14th c. and stands on five columns. A stone coffin lies on the
floor of the west end. There is a simple 16th c. parish chest. The rood
screen is splendid and undamaged. The rood stairs are still open. In
the chancel there is a double aumbry and a large trefoil piscina.

ICKLINGHAM

Dedication:	St James
No of Bells:	1
Deanery 1836:	Fordham
Hundred:	Lackford
Union house:	Mildenhall
Deanery 2000:	Mildenhall

3¾ miles SE of Mildenhall between Barton Mills & Lackford on the A1101 on a bend near the entrance to the flour mill.
O.S. grid ref: TL 770730
Post Code: IP28 6PS

In stark contrast to All Saints at the other end of the village (page 112) this church is dead and uninteresting, but we must be thankful that the Victorians turned their attentions here and not to All Saints. The church is crowded in by trees, shrubs and a factory. It is suffocating. Inside, I had the same impression. There is a stoup just inside the south door and an aumbry in the north wall of the north aisle. The holy table has some notable tracery. The other fittings are run of the mill and uninteresting, The rood screen has been ripped out and parts of it have been incorporated into the modern benches. What may delight the visitor however is the 14th c. parish chest which belonged to All Saints and is completely covered in ironwork, and has a secret device to conceal the keyhole.

ICKWORTH

Dedication:	St Mary
No of Bells:	1
Deanery 1836:	Thingoe
Hundred:	Thingoe
Union house:	Bury St Edmunds
Deanery 2000:	Thingoe

3 miles SW of Bury St Edmunds on the Ickworth Estate, only accessible by visiting Ickworth Hall by way of the National Trust.
O.S. grid ref: TL 812611
Post Code: IP29 5QE

Derelict and uncared for! A mausoleum to the Hervey family, and a sorry remnant of the glorious church this once was. The Herveys once made themselves responsible for the upkeep of many west Suffolk churches, most notably Horringer, Westley and Chevington, and they financed the building of St John's in Bury St Edmunds. They also promised to look after this one. How things have changed! This is the only Suffolk church that you actually have to pay to see and it is heart-breaking. Although the National Trust manages only the house and grounds, a fee is payable on entrance to the Park at Horringer. At the moment the font and piscina remain in the church, and the bells still hang in the belfry. It isn't too late to rescue this once proud and lovely church. The N.T. has no liability to the church.

INGHAM

Dedication:	St Bartholomew
No of Bells:	5
Deanery 1836:	Blackbourn
Hundred:	Blackbourn
Union house:	Bury St Edmunds
Deanery 2000:	Ixworth

4 miles N of Bury St Edmunds between Brockley & Ampton, on the A134 through the village directly on The Street.

O.S. grid ref: TL 855705

Post Code: IP31 1NQ

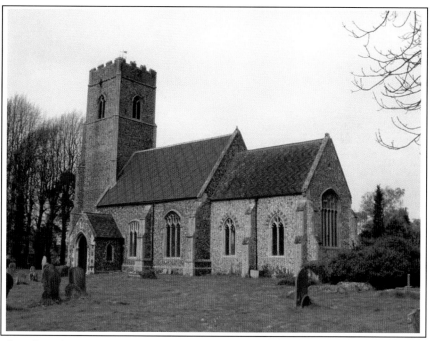

The church sits very close to the busy A134 but is shielded from it by a few trees. It is the sort of church one could find scaled down on a model railway. Typical of what one would expect a church to be: neat porch, red roofs, a well-proportioned tower with a crenulated parapet. The only thing missing is the sound of the bells ringing across the fields on a Sunday morning. This church has very little to offer the visitor except a quiet place to sit and reflect on how many have passed through its doors in the last 900 years. The font is the most interesting object, a very late 12th c. square bowl on a round shaft. Some of the fragments of 15th c. glass in the windows, I am told, are worthy of closer inspection. The carved wooden panels on the pulpit and four poppy-heads may make a visit worthwhile.

IXWORTH

Dedication:	St Mary	
No of Bells:	6	
Deanery 1836:	Blackbourn	
Hundred:	Blackbourn	
Union house:	Bury St Edmunds	
Deanery 2000:	Ixworth	

7 miles NE of Bury St Edmunds between Bury & Stanton. Turn off the A143 at the roundabout, southern end of The High Street.
O.S. grid ref: TL 931703
Post Code: IP31 2HH

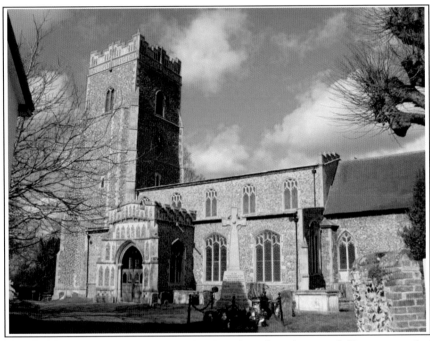

Set back off the street is this lovely church, partially concealed behind a high wall. By the path is the war memorial. The porch is late 14th c. and quite tall, with what I think is a lamb on one side of the arch and a wolf on the other. The tower is 15th c. and has a crenulated parapet. The clerestory and nave roof are 16th c.. The font is octagonal from top to bottom with small engaged columns around the shaft. Probably the oldest thing you will see is the early 13th c. piscina. It has a double arch with a central column. Next to it is the dropped-sill sedilia. The monuments are worthy of mention. The most elaborate is the altar tomb complete with brasses to Richard Coddington (1567) and Elizabeth, his wife. The pulpit has some nice linen-fold carving and there is a small selection of carved bench ends.

IXWORTH THORPE

Dedication:	All Saints
No of Bells:	1
Deanery 1836:	Blackbourn
Hundred:	Blackbourn
Union house:	Bury St Edmunds
Deanery 2000:	Ixworth

2 miles N of Ixworth
between Ixworth &
Honington, on the A1088
Thetford Road, almost
opposite Manor Farm.
O.S. grid ref: TL 917725
Post Code: IP31 1QH

This is one of Suffolk's sporadic thatched churches. It lost its tower many centuries ago and the present base is built from the remains of the upper stages. Today it is topped by a wooded belfry stage containing a single bell. Whilst the church is Norman, the porch which protects the small doorway is Tudor. It has flint decoration in red brick and has pinnacles from the fallen tower at the corners. The 14th c. font is very stark and without decoration and has a crude boarded Stuart cover. The minimal pulpit is also Stuart. Many of the notorious 15th c. carved bench ends are carved on one side only, suggesting they were placed against a wall in their past life. The Royal Arms are those of George III. A copy of 'The Degrees of Marriage' hang in the church and are said to be the best in Suffolk.

KEDINGTON *****

Dedication:	Sts Peter & Paul	
No of Bells:	5 + 1 clock bell	
Deanery 1836:	Clare	
Hundred:	Risbridge	
Union house:	Haverhill	
Deanery 2000:	Clare	

3 miles NE of Haverhill between Great Wratting & Sturmer, Essex. From the A1061 turn east onto Mill Road and follow 500 yds. O.S. grid ref: TL 705470 Post Code: CB9 7NN

Roman remains and a Saxon cross have been discovered, and it was here too the Normans built their church. The Victorians largely left the later mediaeval church alone. On the east face of the 14th c. tower the old roofline can be clearly seen, indicating that the nave roof has been renewed. That happened in the 16th c. and a false hammerbeam roof was constructed. Despite 19th c. skylights it is dim inside, but here you will find splendid things to see. The font is 15th c., the 14th c. chancel has a mutilated piscina, but the monuments to the Barnardiston family are spectacular. Stone and marble life size effigies are scattered liberally throughout the nave and chancel. Wall monuments with heraldic devices stretch from floor to ceiling. It is impossible to describe everything, so go and see for yourself.

KENNY HILL

		5 miles NW of Mildenhall
Dedication:	St James	between Beck Row &
No of Bells:	1	Shippea Hill Stn, Cambs,
Deanery 1836:	part of Mildenhall	on the A1101 opposite
Hundred:	part of Mildenhall	Kenny Hill Drove.
Union house:	part of Mildenhall	O.S. grid ref: TL 668797
Deanery 2000:	Mildenhall	Post Code: IP28 8DS

Kenny Hill is a relatively new parish which was once a hamlet of Mildenhall. The church was built in 1895 and replaced a temporary, 19 year old iron clad structure. It was built in the style of an Early-English church and of traditional flint and stone. The symbolic tower is octagonal from the bottom with a conical cap above the belfry. H. Munro Cautley likened it to a sharpened lead pencil. The alignment is northeast-southwest with the small entrance porch set in the latter. Inside the three-bay nave there is nothing of interest. The narrow chancel contains nothing more than the basic accoutrements for conducting a service. It was declared redundant in the 1970s and was bought by Evangelists who still use it as a Sunday school. It is open weekdays, 10 am to 3 pm, if you are sufficiently curious.

KENTFORD

		5 miles NE of Newmarket
Dedication:	St Mary	between Moulton &
No of Bells:	3	Herringswell, on the
Deanery 1836:	Clare	B1506 , Bury Rd between
Hundred:	Risbridge	the two crossroads.
Union house:	Mildenhall	O.S. grid ref: TL 706667
Deanery 2000:	Mildenhall	Post Code: CB8 7PT

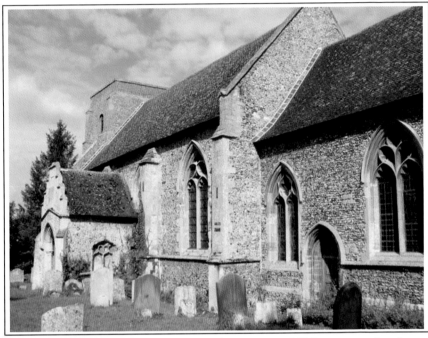

This church was built around the time Henry VIII was on the throne and the dissolution of the monasteries was taking place. It has changed very little since, apart from some minor restoration in 1871. The tower is little more than a stump, having fallen centuries ago. When the tower was rebuilt a small rose window was inserted into the west face, not something one would expect to find in a tower. Inside the porch, with its attractive crow-stepped gable, you will find a locked door. Inside the nave traces of paintings can be seen on the north wall. The careful observer should be able to make out the three figures wearing crowns. They are the 'three quick and the three dead'. Quite a rarity. The seating is in the form of 18th c. box pews which are said to be the best examples in Suffolk.

120

KERSEY ****

Dedication:	St Mary
No of Bells:	6
Deanery 1836:	Sudbury
Hundred:	Cosford
Union house:	Semer
Deanery 2000:	Hadleigh

2 miles NW of Hadleigh
between Hadleigh & Semer
from the A1071 to the
A1141. First left into the
village, at the sharp bend.
O.S. grid ref: TM 002439
Post Code: IP7 6EF

Everyone has heard of Kersey and seen the church on the hill in the background of pictures of the ford which runs across the road. Very few visit the church. It has a large car park and a lychgate to welcome you. There was a church here in 1086 but today's edifice is 14th c. The tower with its attractive parapet stage and porch being built a century later. The font is 15th c. with quatrefoil decoration. Above, the nave roof has alternating hammerbeams with figures carved into them. In the Sampson chapel the piscina and incorporated triple sedilia are richly carved in great detail. Six panels of the old rood screen with painted figures are in very good condition for their age. There is much to see here and it is worth a visit. It only just falls short of achieving my five-star recommendation. I'll give it four!

KETTLEBASTON

Dedication:	St Mary
No of Bells:	3
Deanery 1836:	Sudbury
Hundred:	Cosford
Union house:	Semer
Deanery 2000:	Lavenham

7 miles NW of Hadleigh between Lavenham & Hitcham, at the south end of the village set slightly back from the road.
O.S. grid ref: TL 965502
Post Code: IP7 7QA

When I visited on a beautiful summer afternoon the bazaar had just finished and the tables were being cleared. This, I thought, is obviously a well loved church. The church has Norman origins and a slit window in the north nave wall has been blocked. The porch (not the gazebo) protects the 13th c. south doorway. The square font is early 12th c., and stands on four legs, and is roughly decorated with chevron designs. The chancel contains the piscina and matching triple sedilia, all with cusped arches and clustered columns. A second piscina is in the north wall of the nave. A small niche which has lost its image stool with later painted decoration is another sign of the early origins of the church. There is an Easter sepulchre at the division of the chancel and sanctuary.

KNETTISHALL

Dedication:	All Saints	
No of Bells:	3	
Deanery 1836:	Blackbourn	
Hundred:	Blackbourn	
Union house:	Thetford	
Deanery 2000:	Rockland, Norfolk	

7 miles E of Thetford
between Rushford, Norfolk
& Hopton All Saints, ½
mile south of Gasthorpe,
Norfolk. Private residence.
O.S. grid ref: TL 972802
Post Code: IP22 2TJ

This is now a private residence. I didn't find anyone at home so I rely on H. Munro Cautley for the earlier history of the building. Cautley recorded in 1933 that the church was in a fearful state. The tower had a flint panelled parapet displaying the crowned letters ST and SM. Many of the fittings had already been transferred to Riddlesworth just over the Norfolk border. Knettishall is one of the few Norfolk parishes situated in Suffolk. The 15th c. font has been moved to Lakenham St Alban's in Norwich. The piscina was 14th c. and was flanked by a dropped sill sedilia. The church later fell into ruins and was thankfully rebuilt into the edifice we see today. I congratulate the builder in reconstructing the church as it is today, enriching the otherwise bleak east Breckland landscape.

LACKFORD

Dedication:	St Lawrence
No of Bells:	1
Deanery 1836:	Thingoe
Hundred:	Thingoe
Union house:	Bury St Edmunds
Deanery 2000:	Thingoe

6 miles NW of Bury St Eds between Icklingham & Fornham from the A1101. Turn into housing complex and down Holden Road.
O.S. grid ref: TL 797702
Post Code: IP28 6HZ

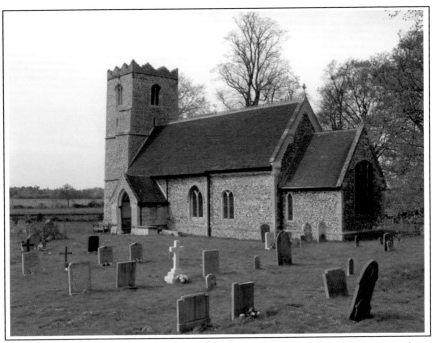

Leave your car at the end of Holden Road and walk the 250 yards to the church. The church was originally Norman but was restructured in the 14th c. but over-zealous restorers have been active since. Nevertheless it is quite an attractive structure. The 15th c. brick parapet on the 14th c. tower is certainly unusual. A tiny chancel is the earliest part of the church, being 13th c. In Puritan times the late 13th c. font was preserved by being plastered over, covering the religious icons. The piscina and sedilia are about the same date. In the recess is a grinning mask. Against the wall is a coped stone coffin lid with 13th c decoration. Some old bench ends are marked with interesting scratchings and graffiti. Very near to Lackford Lakes, make a day of it, and spend a few minutes here.

LAKENHEATH *****

Dedication:	St Mary
No of Bells:	5
Deanery 1836:	Fordham
Hundred:	Lackford
Union house:	Mildenhall
Deanery 2000:	Mildenhall

10 miles W of Thetford
between Mildenhall &
Hockwold, Norfolk, un-
missable on the B1112
Lakenheath High Street.
O.S. grid ref: TL 714827
Post Code: IP27 2DS

There is much of interest here. The building was started in the 13th c.
H. Munro Cautley believes that at the west of the tower there is a
16th c. Galilee porch, above which was possibly a guild chapel. The
font is 13th c. and is regarded as the best in the county. It is certainly
a very impressive heavily carved bowl sitting on eight columns,
crowned by a superb cover. Probably the most unusual thing visitors
are likely to see are the bench end carvings. Some are very risqué, all
are carefully executed. The leopard and the mirror, and the circle of
life are the most unusual. The 14th c. wall paintings on the north
arcade are superb. Look up at the magnificent roof and admire the
craftsmanship that went into its construction. There is much more to
see here but space will not permit me more detail. See for yourself.

125

LANGHAM

Dedication:	St Mary
No of Bells:	2
Deanery 1836:	Blackbourn
Hundred:	Blackbourn
Union house:	Onehouse
Deanery 2000:	Ixworth

9 miles NE of Bury St Edmunds between Walsham le Willows & Stowlangtoft. See main text for directions.

O.S. grid ref: TL980690

Post Code: IP31 3EE

The church stands in the grounds of Langham Hall. To reach it, be prepared to walk across the meadow in which it stands. Start your journey from OS map ref: 596687, or post code IP31 3EG near Hall Farm and the little stream nearby. The church will probably be locked and there is no notice regarding a keyholder. There is no tower but the double bell turret looks right for the church. A niche in the eastern face of the northwest nave buttress seems without purpose. The font is 14th c. and is decorated with heraldic shields. Set into the east wall either side of the holy table is a canopied niche with ogee arch and crocketted finials. These date to around the 14th c. which is contemporary with the building of the church. There has been some mid-Victorian restoration work.

LAVENHAM *****
Dedication: Sts Peter & Paul
No of Bells: 8
Deanery 1836: Sudbury
Hundred: Babergh
Union house: Semer
Deanery 2000: Lavenham

5 miles NE of Sudbury
between Long Melford &
Monks Eleigh.
Unmissable in the village
centre.
O.S. grid ref: TL 912490
Post Code: CO10 9RZ

So much has been written about this beautiful church, probably more than any other in Suffolk. There is much to see and I commend it to the reader. It is late 15th c. and built with the profits from the wool trade. The chief financiers were the Earl of Oxford and Thomas Spryng, a clothier and wool merchant. Virtually the whole building is built from dressed stone, whereas the 140 feet high tower is of the more common dressed flint and stone. The church is 173 feet long by 68 feet wide; the nave is 43 feet high. The 14th c. purbeck font is the oldest item you will see here. Dr. Henry Copinger's monument is in the chancel. On the misericordes the carvings are rich and varied. The screens, rood and parclose, are intricately carved, the former being older than the church. Be sure to see the lovely 'baby brass'.

LAWSHALL

Dedication:	All Saints	
No of Bells:	6	
Deanery 1836:	Sudbury	
Hundred:	Blackbourn	
Union house:	Onehouse	
Deanery 2000:	Sudbury	

7 miles S of Bury St Eds between Hartest & Bradfield Combust, on the north side of The Street you pass through the village.
O.S. grid ref: TL 864542
Post Code: IP29 4QA

There is not very much to interest the visitor here, but it is a striking building. The tower is well proportioned and has clock-faces above the belfry chamber. The nave with its clerestory lights up the interior, especially when the sun shines. The roof is of cambered tie-beam construction. When the Victorian chancel was built a new piscina and two sedilia were incorporated. I was surprised to see that the lovely old 15th c. font had been painted to match the cornice and angels below the clerestory windows. The altar rail seems to have suffered the same regrettable fate. In my opinion, that is not the best approach to brightening up a church. There are two chests, one inlaid, about 17th c., the other plain mahogany with ornamental brass embellishments and lock-plate.

LAYHAM

Dedication:	St Andrew
No of Bells:	1
Deanery 1836:	Sudbury
Hundred:	Cosford
Union house:	Semer
Deanery 2000:	Hadleigh

1½ miles S of Hadleigh between Hadleigh & Raydon. From the B1070 in Upper Layham go to Lower Layham. On a 3-crossways O.S. grid ref: TM 030403 Post Code: IP7 5LZ

The church serves both Upper and Lower Layham. It seems to crouch like a hare in a meadow, ready to take flight; the result of the roofline being low pitched and the red brick tower having no real height. A scratch dial has been re-positioned low down on the east side of the nave buttress during restoration in the 1860s. Inside the church, the lovely traditional style 13th c. hexagonal purbeck marble font is standing on a modern base, supported by six marble columns around a central shaft. In the chancel, the 19th c. reredos is a fine piece of the stonemason's art, with tiled niches, crocketted pinnacles and colourful paintings. In the south west wall of the nave there is a dole shelf, which was once used to hand out bread to the poor. There is a painted panel memorial to Ann Roane (1626) worth a close look.

129

LEAVENHEATH

Dedication: St Matthew
No of Bells: 1
Deanery 1836: Sudbury
Hundred: Babergh
Union house: Sudbury
Deanery 2000: Hadleigh

6 miles WSW of Hadleigh between Newton & Nayland, easily missed, on the A134, half-way up the hill nr Church Cottages.
O.S. grid ref: TL 954371
Post Code: nr CO6 4PW

Set back from the road this church is ugly from the outside, and could be taken for a house if it wasn't for the tower. Inside the church is the same although it is clean, cared for and functional. There is a shortage of natural light which does not show off the interior to best effect. The red brick walls and pillars give it a quite up-to-date appearance. Originally built in the 1830s with Tudor-Gothic detail, it was enlarged in the 1880s and the strange-looking tower was added at the same time. The doorway arch is in stone, trying to look traditional, but the spirelet on top of the tiled pyramidal roof is pitiable. It is not what one would expect a Victorian church to look like, and is very different from any other contemporary church in Suffolk. For that reason it is interesting, but not my cup of tea.

LIDGATE

Dedication:	St Mary	
No of Bells:	5	
Deanery 1836:	Clare	
Hundred:	Risbridge	
Union house:	Exning	
Deanery 2000:	Clare	

7 miles SE of Newmarket
between Wickhambrook &
Ashley, north of the village
on the B1063, accessible
from The Street, turn north.
O.S. grid ref: TL 720581
Post Code: CB8 9PT

This was originally a Norman church. It has been suggested that the chancel was perhaps the chapel to the Norman castle, only a few yards away. It was almost certainly the site of it. The chancel, which is unusually taller than the nave, has 13th c. lancet windows. Everything else in the church is of a later date. The font which is octagonal and very plain is 15th c., but the pyramidal cover is Stuart, as is the octagonal pulpit. The double piscina with cusped arch is early 14th c. which might suggest a rebuilding phase about that period, as the castle fell into decline. North of the chancel is a double aumbry. The north aisle contains a late 15th c. parclose screen. On the pillars of the arcade you will find some mediaeval graffiti including a caricature and musical notations.

131

LINDSEY

Dedication:	St Peter	
No of Bells:	1	
Deanery 1836:	Sudbury	
Hundred:	Cosford	
Union house:	Semer	
Deanery 2000:	Hadleigh	

3 miles NW of Hadleigh between Chelsworth & Edwardstone, on Church Road, Lindsey. South of Lindsey Tye.
O.S. grid ref: TL 977449
Post Code: IP7 6PS

It was in 1836 that Lindsey church lost its tower, and since then the single bell is contained in a small timbered bellcote. The porch is 14th c. and doesn't look a day less. The gnarled old oak timbers have protected the doorway for almost 600 years. Attached to the arch are two shoe scrapers, a reminder that the roads and paths weren't always as clean as they are today. The church is contemporary with the porch and has changed very little over the intervening years, however all periods of history are represented. It is unusual in that the carving on the 13th c. font is in relief, and a cover larger than today's Stuart example, once hung from a pulley above. The Stuart pulpit has been spoiled by the removal of the sounding board. Half the painted lower part of the rood screen is still in place and can be seen.

LITTLE BRADLEY

Dedication:	All Saints
No of Bells:	1
Deanery 1836:	Clare
Hundred:	Risbridge
Union house:	Haverhill
Deanery 2000:	Clare

5 miles N of Haverhill
between Little Thurlow &
Great Bradley. From the
B1061 turn east near shelter,
signed to Lt. Bradley.
O.S. grid ref: TL 681521
Post Code: CB9 7JD

This lovely little Norman church is a treat to visit. The setting is tranquil and on a sunny afternoon you can imagine yourself back in the 'Good Old Days'. The late Saxon round tower with its later octagonal belfry stage complements the church beautifully. The porch has been virtually rebuilt and it is unfortunate that the restoration of this ancient building was not more sympathetically carried out. The octagonal font which is 14th c. is quite plain and unadorned. Also probably late Saxon in origin is the nave and part of the chancel. Two slit windows on the east wall have been blocked, as has the low side window in the chancel. On the south chancel wall there are also signs of rebuilding. The piscina is set into the splay of the window reveal and is flanked by the dropped-sill sedilia.

LITTLE CORNARD

Dedication:	All Saints
No of Bells:	5
Deanery 1836:	Sudbury
Hundred:	Babergh
Union house:	Sudbury
Deanery 2000:	Sudbury

2 miles SE of Sudbury and S of Great Cornard. From the B1508 turn east up Keddington Hill, signed Lt. Cornard, and continue 1 ml.
O.S. grid ref: TL 901390
Post Code: CO10 0PE

I cannot remember a more overgrown and unloved churchyard than this, except perhaps for Nettlestead, (which lives up to its name). Here nettles were at least six feet tall in places, and the excuse is that it is a nature conservation area. There is little of any architectural or historical interest here; almost everything worthwhile was removed or destroyed during the Victorian restoration. The modified porch seems disproportionate to the size of the church. A lead-covered lantern prevails over the embattled tower. A 15th c. font of simplistic design sits at the west end of the nave. An angel looks sadly down from a 15th c. roundel on the north wall. What appears to be the north aisle is in fact housing the organ, although at one time it was a vestry with a floor above. I think the key was lost years ago.

LITTLE FINBOROUGH

Dedication:	St Mary
No of Bells:	1
Deanery 1836:	Stow
Hundred:	Stow
Union house:	Onehouse
Deanery 2000:	Stowmarket

4 miles SW of Stowmarket between Wattisham & Combs. Turn at right-angle bend to Lt Finborough Hall and follow to destination.
O.S. grid ref: TM 018549
Post Code: IP14 2LE

There has been very little said about this modest church. H. Munro Cautley comments: 'There is nothing of interest in this church but the Arms of George III dated 1767, which hang on the tympanic filling above rood-beam.' That was it! I remember driving up to the church and wondering if I would be able to turn the car round. I could! While I was there, I enjoyed the churchyard's peace and tranquillity. Restoration took place in 1867/8, when the west end was rebuilt. Above the west end of the nave a bellcote was erected which houses a single bell. I don't believe there has ever been a tower here. The church is 14th c. The thatch was removed and the roofs were tiled when restoration took place. The nave and chancel floors were also tiled and new benches put in, with a new pulpit to match.

LITTLE LIVERMERE

Dedication:	Sts Peter & Paul	
No of Bells:	1	
Deanery 1836:	Blackbourn	
Hundred:	Blackbourn	
Union house:	Bury St Edmunds	
Deanery 2000:	Ixworth	

5 miles N of Bury St Edmunds, $^1/_3$ mile N of Great Livermere in the grounds of Park Farm. Visitors are not welcomed.
O.S. grid ref: TL 881718
Post Code: IP31 1LA

This church is inaccessible and probably dangerous. There is very little to see now anyway. A tall tower and a nave full of fifty-year-old trees is a sorry site, but time will move on and one day these ruins may be accessible again and properly managed. This was once an important church. The roof was salvaged in 1947 and the fittings spread among the surrounding churches. Saxon long and short work and Norman windows and doorways were evident. For many years it had been falling into disuse and in the 1930s it was only used for funerals. The squire had his own private entrance to the church and a pew in which he could nod off without being seen by the great unwashed. Even they were herded into horse-box type pews. Perhaps that's why they stopped going to church.

LITTLE SAXHAM

Dedication:	St Nicholas	
No of Bells:	1 + 2 grounded	
Deanery 1836:	Thingoe	
Hundred:	Thingoe	
Union house:	Bury St Edmunds	
Deanery 2000:	Thingoe	

5 miles W of Bury St Edmunds between Bury St Edmunds, & Barrow. Approach from any direction, unmissable.
O.S. grid ref: TL 799637
Post Code: IP29 5LH

Here is the finest example of a Norman tower in the county, and yet it is Saxon at the base. The blind arcading at the belfry stage is something you don't see very often. Another nice example is at Thorington (E. Suffolk. p. 260). The south door is contemporary with the tower. The porch which has a small stoup is 14th c.. Inside, there are two bells which have been removed from the belfry. Notice the Norman hinges on the door to the rood loft stairs. Animals and grotesques are carved on the bench ends. The tomb with the painted shields is that of Thomas Fitz-Lucas (1531). The piscina has a very simple cusped arch and is adjacent to the dropped-sill sedilia. The altar rails are from Little Livermere. The pulpit is Stuart and retains the sounding board, and an old bier has extendable handles.

LITTLE THURLOW

Dedication: St Peter
No of Bells: 5
Deanery 1836: Clare
Hundred: Risbridge
Union house: Haverhill
Deanery 2000: Clare

4 miles N of Haverhill between Great Wratting & Great Bradley. From the B1061 turn east at Pound Green into Church Road.
O.S. grid ref: TL 680511
Post Code: CB9 7JQ

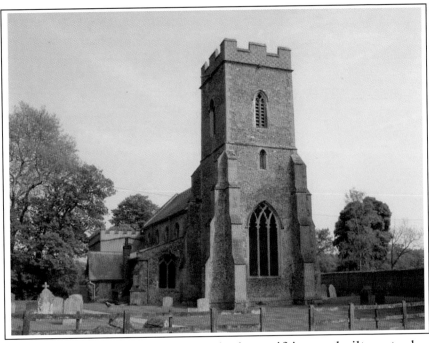

The tower with its six buttresses looks as if it was built yesterday, while the rest of the church looks its age. It is a hotch-potch of add-ons. The clerestory windows are round. Entry is via the north porch, there is no south porch. The font is one of those lovely old square models from the 12th c. with carvings on all four facets. In the south aisle is one of the 13th c. piscinas, complete with credence shelf. In the chancel, you will find a double piscina with moulded arches and a central pillar. The north-east lump on the outside is the Soame chapel; inside it is splendid with the monument of Sir Stephen Soame (1619) housed within. Guarded by railings, it is huge, with various designs styles and figures all over the place. It must have cost an absolute fortune. If you are into monuments, it's a must.

LITTLE WALDINGFIELD

Dedication:	St Lawrence	
No of Bells:	6	
Deanery 1836:	Sudbury	
Hundred:	Babergh	
Union house:	Sudbury	
Deanery 2000:	Sudbury	

4 miles NE of Sudbury between Sudbury & Monks Eleigh. From the B1115 turn into Church Road opposite the Swan Inn.
O.S. grid ref: TL 924451
Post Code: CO10 0SP

Here is a church that does not conform to your expectations. The parish is named 'Little' but the church is imposing and it says. 'I am here, look at me'. And so we shall! There are two pinnacled turret stairs at the east end of the nave, both giving access to the roof. The south porch is stratified red brick and rubble. The 14th c. font is interesting in that the designs are unusual. Look up and you will see the nave roof with its arch-braced and flat cambered tie-beams. Look towards the east and see the beauty of the 16th c. crocketted arcade, and the tall chancel arch. Sunlight spills into the beautiful interior from the clerestory. The Stuart pulpit sits precariously on its pillar. The parish chest with its rusty fastenings is 15th c. and has a traceried front panel. Another chest, circa 1300, is not on display.

LITTLE WHELNETHAM

Dedication:	St Mary Magdalene
No of Bells:	3
Deanery 1836:	Thedwastre
Hundred:	Thedwastre
Union house:	Bury St Edmunds
Deanery 2000:	Lavenham

4 miles SE of Bury St Edmunds, between Sicklesmere & Bradfield St George. From the A134 turn east at Sicklesmere, continue. O.S. grid ref: TL 888600 Post Code: IP30 0DA

At the eastern end of this church you will notice a heap of old stones and rubble. This was the apsidal end of an early Norman church. The present church has migrated westwards. I can imagine a round tower here originally, the remains of which are probably under the nave. Inside the nave you will find an unusual configuration of roof: hammerbeams, with two arch-braced principles where normally there would be only one. The hammerbeams are carved figures looking down and left and right, another unusual feature. The font is a typical 15th c. example but the 12th c. piscina differs from the norm in that it takes the form of a bracket pillar. The lectern too is very different. Carvings on the bench ends are worth investigation. If you are looking for something different, this is where you'll find it.

LITTLE WRATTING

Dedication:	St Mary	
No of Bells:	1	
Deanery 1836:	Clare	
Hundred:	Risbridge	
Union house:	Haverhill	
Deanery 2000:	Clare	

2 miles NE of Haverhill between Haverhill & Barnardiston. From the A143 turn north at the factory and immediate left.
O.S. grid ref: TL 686471
Post Code: CB9 7UG

Have a good look round the exterior of this lovely little Saxon church before you enter. There are not many churches as small and compact as Little Wratting. The wooden bell turret rests on the floor of the nave, not on the roof as one might expect. Inside the 19th c. porch, over the south door you will see a lintel. On it is written in Latin 'DEDICACIO AV...' The name of the saint has been erased or covered. If this was the original Norman dedication stone, I believe it is unique in Suffolk. The chancel and chancel arch have been rebuilt, and a small stoup has been incorporated into the arch. The 14th c. piscina has been put back in its proper place. The font is disappointingly plain and has an octagonal conical cover. You may get there and find the door locked. No keyholder is listed.

LONG MELFORD ***** 3 miles N of Sudbury
Dedication: Holy Trinity between   Alpheton &
No of Bells: 8 Sudbury. Situated north of
Deanery 1836:   Sudbury the village, just off the
Hundred: Babergh A1092 north of The Green.
Union house: Sudbury O.S. grid ref: TL 865467
Deanery 2000:   Sudbury Post Code: CO10 9DT

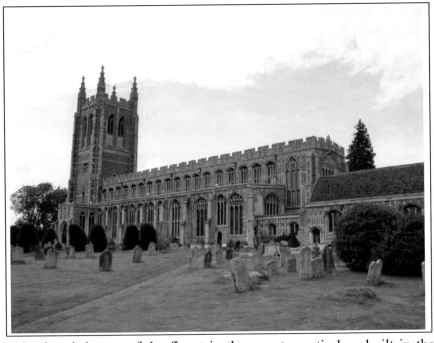

This church is one of the finest in the county, entirely rebuilt in the late 15th c. on the strength of the wool trade. John Clopton (1497) largely supported the enormous cost of the rebuild. The present tower was rebuilt in 1903. The church is about 260 feet long, and about 60 feet wide. There is so much to see here that it is pointless trying to list everything. The font is 15th c. purbeck marble. Magnificent tombs to Sir William Cordell (1580), and to William Clopton (1446) both have life-size effigies along with many others. Brasses are several and various. The roof is a magnificent cambered tie-beam construction with arch braces, and is continuous from west to east. I think the alabaster reredos is the most striking thing I have seen in any Suffolk church. Do go and see for yourself.

MARKET WESTON

Dedication:	St Mary	9 miles ESE of Thetford
No of Bells:	5	between Hopton All Saints
Deanery 1836:	Blackbourn	& Barningham. Turn off the
Hundred:	Blackbourn	B1111 into Church Road,
Union house:	Thetford	Market Weston and follow.
Deanery 2000:	Ixworth	O.S. grid ref: TL 990781

9 miles ESE of Thetford
between Hopton All Saints
& Barningham. Turn off the
B1111 into Church Road,
Market Weston and follow.
O.S. grid ref: TL 990781
Post Code: IP22 2NX

Seemingly planted in the middle of a field this super little church reminds me of Carleton St Peter in Norfolk. It has a south porch with three empty canopied niches. Above the south doorway another canopied niche contains a statuette of St. Mary. Directly facing the south door are the dirtiest Royal Arms of Charles I that I have ever seen. On the facets of the bowl of the octagonal font there is ogee decoration. The roof of the nave is a very light double hammerbeam type and the chancel roof is arch-braced. The piscina is a pillar type with six engaged columns and above the bowl is a stone carving. It is most unusual and I have no idea of its age. Above the tower arch hangs a list of benefactions to the parish of Weston Market which makes interesting reading.

MELLIS

Dedication:	St Mary the Virgin	
No of Bells:	1	
Deanery 1836:	Hartismere	
Hundred:	Hartismere	
Union house:	Eye & Wortham	
Deanery 2000:	Hartismere	

3 miles W of Eye between Eye & Wortham. Situated behind trees, 75 yds off the road, west of the railway line on Mellis Green.
O.S. grid ref: TL 948743
Post Code: IP23 8EE

Finding this church is easier in winter than in summer when the leaves are on the trees. It appears somewhat dilapidated at first sight, with only the rendered remains of the tower which fell in 1730. This obviously was once a handsome church but time has taken its toll. Above the south porch there is a chamber. The Royal Arms of Charles I hang in the blocked tower arch. The restored traditional East Anglian style font has four lions around the base and emblems round the bowl. The piscina is contained in a small plain arch. The rood stairs which rise within the thickness of the wall are still open at the bottom. A mutilated Easter sepulchre is set into the north wall of the sanctuary. Behind the pulpit is a tomb, now devoid of its brasses, but is believed to be that of John Yaxley (1505).

144

MENDLESHAM

Dedication:	St Mary
No of Bells:	5
Deanery 1836:	Hartismere
Hundred:	Hartismere
Union house:	Eye & Wortham
Deanery 2000:	Stowmarket

6 miles NE of Stowmarket between Wetheringset & Cotton, situated on the east side of the village in Church Road.
O.S. grid ref: TM 105657
Post Code: IP14 5SG

Mendlesham church is quite imposing with a very substantial tower, large porches north and south, (the former with crowned lions watching those who enter). The chamber above the porch has been used as the town's armoury since 1593. On display are Tudor and Stuart suits of armour and a few weapons. The church is spacious and the clerestory spills an abundance of light into the nave. The font is octagonal and plain, whereas the cover, made in 1630 and restored in 1908, is a strange design based on two crowns. The pulpit was commissioned at the same time. Benches in the nave have some interesting grotesques carved on the ends. Most also have traceried backs. The roof of the north aisle has a carved cornice and corbels. An old four-wheeled bier and parish chest are on display in the nave.

MILDEN

Dedication:	St Peter	
No of Bells:	1	
Deanery 1836:	Sudbury	
Hundred:	Babergh	
Union house:	Semer	
Deanery 2000:	Lavenham	

6 miles NW of Hadleigh
1 m S of Monks Eleigh.
From the A1141 take the
B1115, W of Monks Eleigh
and follow road signs.
O.S. grid ref: TL 958465
Post Code: IP7 7AF

It won't surprise you to learn that this little church is of Norman origin. There is a Norman doorway to pass through, and a lancet window in the south chancel wall. The square font is 12th c. and is standing on four pillars, none of which matches its neighbour. The roof has large tie-beams and king-posts supporting it. A few steel tie-rods have since been added just to be on the safe side. The pulpit is Stuart and professionally made whereas the benches are rough-hewn DIY jobs and bear the church wardens' names and the date 1685. The surprise here is the effigy to James Alington (1626) who is resting his head on a book, rather than a dog or deer, as so many are. Obviously a man of learning. A past rector, William Burkitt took after him for he is remembered for teaching the children of the poor to read.

MILDENHALL   *****   8½ miles NNW of
Dedication: St Mary   Newmarket between
No of Bells: 8   Worlington & Lakenheath.
Deanery 1836:   Fordham   Situated on the High Street
Hundred: Lackford   in Mildenhall.
Union house: Mildenhall   O.S. grid ref: TL 710746
Deanery 2000:   Mildenhall   Post Code: IP28 7EE

This magnificent church 168 by 65 feet is in the top five in the county. Part of the church, the vestry and the foundations of the chancel, are dated at 1220 and the oldest part of the building. A church has existed on this site since before Domesday. The piscina and sedilia are early 13th c. Construction of the nave and 112 feet tall tower were in the 15th c. although the latter was refaced in 1864. Dating from about 1420 are the north aisle and the porch with a chapel above. The roofs are decorated with angels lacking their wings, and the carvings on the spandrels are exceptional. Cromwell's men damaged most of the angels, and the roof is peppered with lead musket shot. The monuments are large and impressive. The 15th c. font is of purbeck marble. The huge Royal Arms are of George II.

147

MONKS ELEIGH

Dedication: St Peter
No of Bells: 6 + clock bell
Deanery 1836:   Bocking, Essex
Hundred: Babergh
Union house: Semer
Deanery 2000:   Lavenham

6 miles NW of Hadleigh between Lavenham & Bildeston. From the A1141 (The Street) turn into Church Hill at The Green.
O.S. grid ref: TL 966477
Post Code: IP7 7JQ

The tower is the main feature of this 14th c. church. The buttresses are most interesting in that there are eight, which become four at about 12 feet from the parapet. There are grotesque masks before they continue upwards as an octagonal, finally terminating in a finely crocketted pinnacle above the parapet. A spire was added in 1631 but became unsafe and was demolished in 1845 when the bell cage was erected to house the clock bell. Inside the church you are greeted by a 'poor man's box' dated 1636. Above the chancel arch hang the Royal Arms of Queen Anne. The 13th c. square font is simply decorated, with a moulded central shaft and a pillar at each corner. The mediaeval pulpit is 15th c. and one of the few that remain in the county. There is a 16th c. bier with simple carvings on its flanks.

MOULTON

Dedication:	St Peter	
No of Bells:	5	
Deanery 1836:	Bocking, Essex	
Hundred:	Risbridge	
Union house:	Exning	
Deanery 2000:	Mildenhall	

4 miles W of Newmarket between Newmarket & Gazeley off the B1085 (The Street) into Church Road, cross the ford and turn right.
O.S. grid ref: TL 699641
Post Code: CB8 8SG

Moulton is one of those churches you never see unless you are going to it. There is no road passing its doors, and that is its redeeming feature. Peace and tranquillity prevail. There are subtle signs of a 12th c. church which was incorporated into the building of this one during the 16th c. The church has been restored and added to over the centuries, but the 14th c. tower remains as it was built. Inside, it has a stark appearance but there are a few things of interest. Although the ogee cover is 16th c. the font is relatively new and has a floral design. The benches in the choir have carved animals on the ends. However, it is the frieze above the crocketted arcade that has the best carving. It is always a good idea to carry binoculars when visiting churches. Keys are held by three different keyholders.

NAUGHTON

Dedication: St Mary
No of Bells: 1
Deanery 1836: Sudbury
Hundred: Cosford
Union house: Semer
Deanery 2000: Hadleigh

4 miles N of Hadleigh between Great Bricett & Semer, turn S off the B1078 follow signs to Naughton. Church is on The Green. O.S. grid ref: TM 022489 Post Code: IP7 7DA

What a pleasant little church this is in a freshly mown graveyard and recently painted porch. No great aisles to spoil the appearance of this beautifully proportioned building. The porch is 14th c. and has a delicately carved bargeboard. Inside the church the old 14th c. black braced tie-beams and king-posts draw the eye upwards to the whitewashed ceiling. Virtually unchanged by Victorian intervention this is as it was when it was built. Layer upon layer of whitewash has buried any wall paintings that may have been here. The 12th c. font has been set into an alcove in the north wall. Originally square, and similar to the one at Great Bricett, each corner has been removed and is now octagonal. The piscina in the nave is 14th c. and has a cusped arch. The benches are 17th c. although they look older.

NAYLAND

		7½ miles SE of Sudbury
Dedication:	St James	between Sudbury &
No of Bells:	6	Colchester. From the A134
Deanery 1836:	Sudbury	exit near the sluice and
Hundred:	Babergh	follow road to High Street.
Union house:	Sudbury	O.S. grid ref: TL 975342
Deanery 2000:	Hadleigh	Post Code: CO6 4JH

Unfortunately, the outside of some parts of the building have been cement-rendered and not properly maintained. Restoration has been carried out on a tight budget and the overall effect is a scruffy looking church. Enlarged on the strength of the wool trade in the 15th c. it is quite a large edifice. The 14th c. tower, with its easily recognisable modest spire, is almost all original. Inside the nave we find the re-cut octagonal font and a sturdy parish chest. The clerestory's interior is much smarter, spilling in light from its multitude of windows. A large bier stands forlorn below the Royal Arms of William. Mounted into a frame and hanging on the aisle wall are the eight panels of the old rood screen. Behind the altar is a painting by John Constable. There is more, but space prohibits.

NEDGING

Dedication:	St Mary
No of Bells:	2
Deanery 1836:	Sudbury
Hundred:	Cosford
Union house:	Semer
Deanery 2000:	Hadleigh

5 miles N of Hadleigh between Bildeston & Semer. From the B1115 turn off into the village and follow to its centre.

O.S. grid ref: TL 998482

Post Code: IP7 7HJ

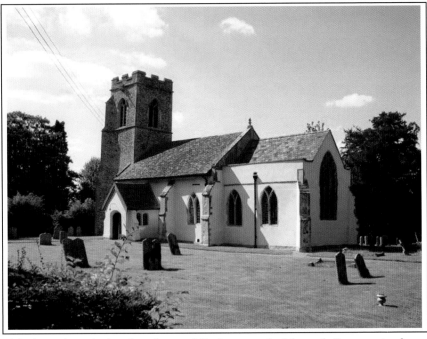

This is a church that has been tidied up, and although I am not a lover of cement-render, this is tasteful and clean. The one thing I object to most strongly is the fact that many of the headstones have been moved from the grave they represent. The church was glad to take the money for the privilege of a headstone. This is vandalism by the PCC. Family historians are horrified to see such sacrilegious actions. Nice Norman doorways invite you into the 13th c. church, which still has the 14th c. king-post that has supported the roof ever since. The 15th c. benches have mutilated carvings on the armrests. The panelling behind the 14th c. dropped-sill sedilia has claimed a few of the others. Unfortunately you will probably not be able to see the treasure of the church, which is the 14th c. 'Dawe' bell in the tower.

NEWMARKET

Dedication: All Saints
No of Bells: 1
Deanery 1836:   Fordham
Hundred: Cheeveley, Cambs
Union house: Exning
Deanery 2000:   Mildenhall

13 miles W of Bury St Edmunds between Ely, Cambs & Haverhill at the junction of All Saints Road & Park Lane, near museum.
O.S. grid ref: TL 644632
Post Code: CB8 8AX

There is a small number of wholly Victorian churches in west Suffolk and include both those in Newmarket. The foundation stone was laid in 1875 on the site of the old church. The design was by Oldham Chambers of Lowestoft, whom Cautley regarded as untutored. The lower part of the tower was preserved and rebuilt to a greater height than before. It is now unsafe for bell-ringing. Noticeable is the fact that the clerestory windows are too small and a poor attempt at Gothic revival. Originally built with an apsidal east end it was remodelled in 1888 to the way it is today. There is nothing of antiquarian interest in the church as nothing was preserved from the old church. It is not even a good example of a late Victorian church. It is however, smart and clean inside with excellent facilities.

NEWMARKET

Dedication:	St Mary	
No of Bells:	5 + 1 clock bell	
Deanery 1836:	Fordham	
Hundred:	Lackford	
Union house:	Exning	
Deanery 2000:	Mildenhall	

13 miles W of Bury St Edmunds between Ely, Cambs & Haverhill off the High Street in Church Lane. Or just off Rowley Drive.
O.S. grid ref: TL 641634
Post Code: CB8 0HP

St Mary's is one of those churches that was stripped of everything, including its character, during the period of Victorian restoration. It is surrounded by other buildings and is unable to show anything except its delicate spire above the rooftops. The destruction started in 1856 when the chancel was rebuilt. The following year a north window was inserted into the chancel. The old galleries were replaced by a new one running the length of the nave. In 1868 the north transept was converted into an aisle and a vestry was added to the north of the chancel. During this period of dissatisfaction with everything, many of the windows were also replaced with 'modern' Victorian versions. The church, unfortunately, has been left with nothing to interest or appeal to the visitor. Perhaps that is why it is kept securely locked.

NEWTON

Dedication: All Saints
No of Bells: 5
Deanery 1836: Sudbury
Hundred: Babergh
Union house: Sudbury
Deanery 2000: Sudbury

3 miles E of Sudbury
between Sudbury &
Boxford. Just off the A134,
N into Church Road at the
Saracen's Head PH.
O.S. grid ref: TL 919412
Post Code: CO10 0QR

This is an early church. Like many Suffolk churches it started life before Domesday. The Normans rebuilt in stone and we see the results here the north doorway, for example, with two engaged columns and an arch with three orders of decoration. It has been blocked and is now a window. Inside the nave the 15th c. font stands on its plinth and is unusual in design and decoration. Nearby is an old bier with wooden spokes to the wheels. On its carriage are photographs showing various aspects of church repairs and updating. The 14th c. double piscina and sedilia are united as one. Margaret Boteler's tomb (1310) and others are worthy of examination, as are the lovely wall-paintings. This is one of the many churches maintained by the Churches Conservation Trust.

NORTON

		6 miles E of Bury St Eds
Dedication:	St Andrew	between Badwell Ash &
No of Bells:	4	Thurston. From the A1088,
Deanery 1836:	Blackbourn	Ixworth Road, turn into The
Hundred:	Blackbourn	Street & into Church Lane.
Union house:	Onehouse	O.S. grid ref: TL 962663
Deanery 2000:	Ixworth	Post Code: IP31 3NB

The great porch and south aisle were added to a diminutive church and are out of proportion from the outside. The Victorians have been at work here too, and this time they seem to have benefited the interior. The early 15th c. font is a delight, a beautifully carved bowl with ecclesiastical emblems; on the corbel are angels, and around the base a lion is engaging a wodewose. You must not miss the ends of the 14th c. stalls which are carved with some unusual scenes. The misericordes too are interesting, including the depiction of the martyrdom of St Edmund. The 15th c. bench ends have buttressed arm rests and more carvings. The 13th c. chest is a treasure and so too is the glass in the windows. Normally I consider glass too specialized to mention, but here it is exceptional. No keyholder.

NOWTON

Dedication:	St Peter	
No of Bells:	6	
Deanery 1836:	Thingoe	
Hundred:	Thingoe	
Union house:	Bury St Edmunds	
Deanery 2000:	Thingoe	

3 miles S of Bury St Eds between Sicklesmere & Horringer. Turn off the A134 near Nowton Park & towards Nowton Hall.

O.S. grid ref: TL 863604

Post Code: IP29 5NF

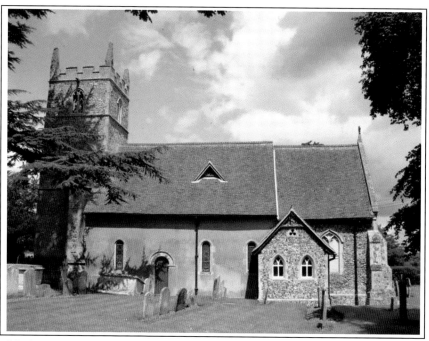

This is another of our churches which is part of our Norman heritage. Unfortunately it has, like many others, been 'got at' by our Victorian ancestors. The strange little dormers in the roof are their doing. The north and south doorways and possibly a slit window in the north wall are Norman. Inside the church all is pristine and clinical. There are two nice canopied niches either side of the altar. The piscina and dropped-sill sedilia match well with the reredos with its cusped arches. The font is a hideous triple-colour marble 'off the peg' job. A monument on the wall to Elizabeth Oakes (1811) has the amended inscription '..in the works of Faith Pope and Charity'. By whose hand, I wonder? The glass is all Flemish picture glass acquired by the husband of the above from monasteries.

OAKLEY

Dedication:	St Nicholas the Great	
No of Bells:	6	
Deanery 1836:	Hartismere	
Hundred:	Hartismere	
Union house:	Eye & Worthing	
Deanery 2000:	Hartismere	

3 miles N of Eye between Hoxne & Stuston. Either in or just west of Oakley turn south into and follow into Oakley Church Lane.
O.S. grid ref: TM 157773
Post Code: IP21 4BW

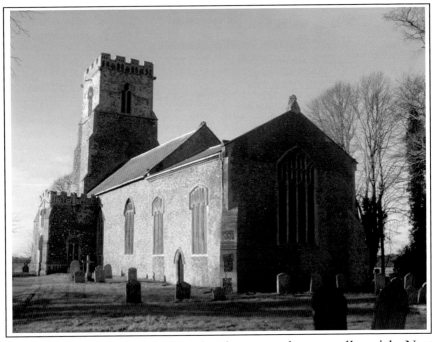

A relatively large church for what is now quite a small parish. Neat and well constructed, the walls have little need for buttressing. The 14th c. tower with its trim embattled parapet dominates the churchyard. The porch, built 100 years later, has some excellent flushwork. There are three niches, the uppermost between a pair of windows in what was the upper chamber. Inside the church there is little of historical interest. The octagonal font is plain and so are the benches, except for one or two poppyheads. It is nice to see that the rood loft stairs have been restored instead of blocked, very refreshing! Close by, there are two nicely decorated image stools set into the wall. It is a shame they are empty, even a posy of flowers would help to brighten up the interior.

OCCOLD

		2 miles S of Eye between
Dedication:	St Michael	Eye & Bedingfield. From
No of Bells:	5	the B1077 turn east into
Deanery 1836:	Hartismere	Occold Street and continue
Hundred:	Hartismere	300 yds to the church.
Union house:	Eye & Wortham	O.S. grid ref: TM 155708
Deanery 2000:	Hartismere	Post Code: IP23 7PD

The church has Norman origins but little remains to be seen. A slit window in the north wall is partially covered by the wall of the 'new' vestry. On the south side, there is a lovely hood-mould over the chancel window. There is little else to see outside except the SE buttress, which is parting company with the tower. A rather plain font is awaiting a carver; the cover is in the form of a crown. The Royal Arms are of Charles II and the lion is straight from Oz. Behind the lovely old richly carved (1620) pulpit, complete with sounding board, is a 14th c. piscina. There are four traceried panels that probably once formed part of the rood screen. In the sanctuary is a single stall with a misericorde. Nearby is the piscina with cusped arch and a somewhat expected dropped-sill style sedilia.

OLD NEWTON

Dedication:	St Mary	
No of Bells:	5	
Deanery 1836:	Stow	
Hundred:	Stow	
Union house:	Onehouse	
Deanery 2000:	Stowmarket	

2 miles N of Stowmarket between Haughley & Mendlesham. From the B1113 turn east at the crossroads, to Church Road. O.S. grid ref: TM 059624 Post Code: IP14 4PP

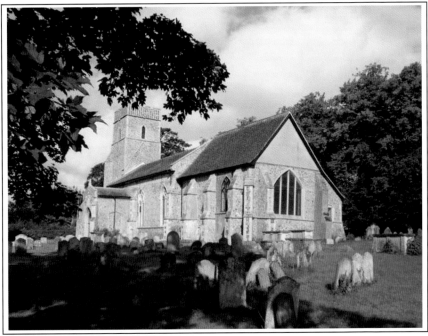

The one thing that stood out here for me was the buttressing on the chancel. Someone was not taking any chances! The church dates back to the 15th c. and is beginning to show its age. Six feet higher than today's apex, the old roof-line is clearly seen on the tower. The 14th c. tracery of the windows is of quite exceptional quality. Those who seek out scratch dials may find a very feint one on one of the nave buttresses. The font is the traditional East Anglian type with lions and wodewoses but has been badly knocked about. Two niches in the east wall of the chancel were uncovered last century. These were discovered during restoration work, which also revealed a sedilia in the south wall of the chancel. The Royal Arms are of George II. Pleasant, but not much to see, even from the new gallery.

ONEHOUSE

Dedication:	St John the Baptist	
No of Bells:	2	
Deanery 1836:	Stow	
Hundred:	Stow	
Union house:	Onehouse	
Deanery 2000:	Stowmarket	

2 miles W of Stowmarket between Rattlesden & Stowmarket. From Forest Road in west of the village turn S into unmade lane.
O.S. grid ref: TM 016593
Post Code: IP14 3EW

The tower was once half as tall again as it is now, but it became unsafe and was reduced to the present height. There is the base of an old cross in the churchyard. A scratch dial can be found on the south wall and there is a small stoup inside the porch. Inside the nave the plaster has been stripped from the walls in places. I don't know if this is permanent as at Iken, (E. Suffolk. p. 140) or marks repairs in progress. The roundish 12th c. font is rough and ready and the faces, with arms outstretched at the quarters, are almost worn away. It sits on a square shaft and plinth. One bench end has a snarling mongrel as an armrest, but there is very little else of interest, unfortunately. If only the walls could speak they would obviously have a wonderful story to tell. You can sense the history, but it is invisible to our eyes.

OUSDEN

Dedication:	St Peter	
No of Bells:	5	
Deanery 1836:	Clare	
Hundred:	Risbridge	
Union house:	Exning	
Deanery 2000:	Clare	

7 miles ESE of Newmarket between Dalham & Depden, west of the village on the Cheveley Road. Turn south by Ousden House.
O.S. grid ref: TL 735595
Post Code: CB8 8TN

This church is a rarity. It was built by the Normans and has a central tower which is original apart from the parapet. The belfry stage has engaged columns carved into the corner stones. The south doorway into the nave (now a window) has a chip-carved lintel, above which is a chequered tympanum. I believe the arch utilises Roman brick. Inside the church, the choir stalls are within the tower arches. The octagonal font is 14th c. and has a waisted shaft of clustered columns. The Royal Arms are Hanoverian. On the wall of the tower arch there is a memorial to Leticia Mosley (1619) with a grisly skeleton but a beautifully worded obituary, worth a moment of your time. Another monument with three cusped blind arches is to the Ireland family members who died in the late 19th century.

PAKENHAM

Dedication:	St Mary
No of Bells:	5
Deanery 1836:	Thedwastre
Hundred:	Thedwastre
Union house:	Bury St Edmunds
Deanery 2000:	Ixworth

5 miles ENE of Bury St Edmunds between Great Barton & Stowlangtoft. Turn off the A143 or A1088 to Pakenham & Church Hill. O.S. grid ref: TL 930670 Post Code: IP31 2LN

This is another Norman church with a central tower (see p 162). In 1849 it was much restored and made into a full cruciform church. Despite the lower part being square, the belfry stage of the tower is octagonal and was built in the 14th c. There are two simple Norman doorways, and some 13th c. stone coffin lids have been leant against the outer wall of the transept. Built into the wall of the nave is a stone coffin. It is not known by the author whether this was an intramural burial or just the convenient use of a large piece of stone. I favour the former, probably someone who died during construction. Inside the church there is a fine 15th c. font with four monks supporting the shaft. The cover is tall and modern. At one time, a doom was painted above the chancel arch, but only a drawing of it remains today.

PALGRAVE

Dedication:	St Peter	4 miles NW of Eye between Diss, Norfolk & Wortham.
No of Bells:	8	From Diss or the A143
Deanery 1836:	Hartismere	follow road-signs to
Hundred:	Hartismere	Palgrave, unmissable.
Union house:	Eye & Wortham	O.S. grid ref: TM 115785
Deanery 2000:	Hartismere	Post Code: IP22 1AG

The church stands right beside the road within its walled graveyard. The tower is late 13th c. and the construction of the nave seems to have followed immediately after. The porch, although restored is a good example of flint and stone flushwork. Each of the three niches has a canopy and a George and Dragon appears in the spandrels of the doorway. On entering the nave there is the breast-plate of a suit of armour hanging above your head, but your eye may be drawn to the hammerbeam roof, of which every part has been painted. It is not colourful as is the roof at Huntingfield, (E. Suffolk. p. 139) but well accomplished nevertheless. The lovely old West Country style font is 12th c. Norman and unique in Suffolk. It has a face at each corner and sits on four columns and a central shaft.

POLSTEAD

Dedication:	St Mary	
No of Bells:	6	
Deanery 1836:	Sudbury	
Hundred:	Babergh	
Union house:	Semer	
Deanery 2000:	Hadleigh	

4 miles SW of Hadleigh between Leavenheath & Shelly, west of the village, just off Water Lane in Polstead.
O.S. grid ref: TL 989380
Post Code: CO6 5BS

Here again is a Norman church that still has much of its original fabric intact. Before venturing inside, look at the original 14th c. mediaeval stone spire. You won't see another anywhere in the county. There are stone spires, but all are reconstructed or Victorian add-ons. Above the priest's door, a Norman window has been blocked. The unusual roof configuration is reflected inside where the great tiebeams and kingposts support it. The brick arches in turn are supported by piers with engaged columns. Dormer windows in the roof admit light. I have never before seen a font built from bricks. It is said to be 13th c.; the five columns that support the bowl certainly are. Don't miss the beautiful Norman west doorway with four orders of decoration only visible from inside the tower.

POSLINGFORD

Dedication:	St Mary
No of Bells:	5
Deanery 1836:	Clare
Hundred:	Risbridge
Union house:	Haverhill
Deanery 2000:	Clare

6 miles ENE of Haverhill between Hundon & Cavendish. Situated beside The Street in the village, opposite the Post Office.
O.S. grid ref: TL 769481
Post Code: CO10 8QY

The church stands close to the road but can easily go unnoticed The churchyard is tidy but sterile. The redbrick south porch has a stoup, three niches and a crow step gable. Inside the porch, the Norman doorway has a tympanum carved with a floral design. The north doorway and the slit window in the nave are all of the same period. The originally square font is also 12th c. but has been reduced in size and the decoration removed. On the wall are the Royal Arms of James I. There is a picture of the doom that once occupied the tympanic filling of the chancel arch. It was destroyed in 1881. The piscina, which has a double cusped ogee arch and an opening into the dropped-sill sedilia, is 14th c. but has been restored. There is an interestingly carved parish chest in the tower. Locked, no keyholder.

PRESTON	****	7 miles NE of Sudbury
Dedication:	St Mary	and directly N of Brent
No of Bells:	6	Eleigh. Situated south of
Deanery 1836:	Sudbury	The Street, at the four
Hundred:	Babergh	cross-ways.
Union house:	Semer	O.S. grid ref: TL 946502
Deanery 2000:	Lavenham	Post Code: CO10 9NQ

The welcome here is genuine with a cup of tea and biscuits offered. Well done Preston! The porch through which you enter the church has panels of flushwork and canopied niches of the finest quality. Inside the church there is a profusion of poppyheads of unusual design, not old but refreshingly different. The Decalogue board is the oldest in the county. Nearby are the splendid Royal Arms of Elizabeth I, another rarity, with a pre-unicorn dragon. The font is another treasure; unusual in the design it carries on the four sides, it is Norman in origin, standing on its four candy-twist columns and central shaft. The piscina is a century later and has the main cusped arch, and a smaller one opening into the adjacent dropped-sill sedilia. For a small church, I happily it give four stars for effort and interest.

RATTLESDEN

		5 miles W of Stowmarket,
Dedication:	St Nicholas	on the Stowmarket to
No of Bells:	6	Felsham road, situated in
Deanery 1836:	Thedwastre	the High Street in the centre
Hundred:	Thedwastre	of the village.
Union house:	Onehouse	O.S. grid ref: TL 978590
Deanery 2000:	Lavenham	Post Code: IP30 0RA

This is an appealing church and very large for the size of the parish. It was virtually rebuilt on the proceeds of the wool trade from the 13th c. foundations of an earlier church. The tower was begun in the 14th c. and completed to its present height in the 15th c. The lovely broached spire is clad with wooden shingles and replaces an earlier one which collapsed. Even the 15th c. south porch originally had wall paintings. The nave has a splendid double hammerbeam roof and sixty-six angels look down from the hammers. The highly decorated late 14th c. font is a mason's masterpiece. The decoration is mostly floral but has faces round the base of the huge octagonal bowl. Some very different poppyheads are also worthy of close examination. Lots to see here and well worth a visit.

REDE

Dedication: All Saints
No of Bells: 3
Deanery 1836: Thingoe
Hundred: Thingoe
Union house: Bury St Edmunds
Deanery 2000: Clare

7 miles SW of Bury St
Edmunds, between Bury
and Haverhill. Turn south
in Chedburgh, follow into
Rede. 40 yds from L bend.
O.S. grid ref: TL 804559
Post Code: IP29 4BE

This lonely little church sits in a pleasant situation in the village centre, set back a little from the road. The tower was built in the early 14th c. at the same time as the church, which has since been partially re-built and the roofs tiled. The porch is a memorial to Arthur J. H. Turner who died July 19th 1877. We know this because it is written on the gable, in the centre of which is a statuette in an ornate niche. The whole church has lost its interest, for historian and architect alike, due to being over-restored. Goblins look down from the tower buttresses. There is little to see inside the church except for a few poppyheads on some old benches. The Stuart pulpit is fairly ordinary as is the plain octagonal font. One old corner bench sits unused at the west end of the nave.

REDGRAVE

Dedication:	St Mary
No of Bells:	6
Deanery 1836:	Hartismere
Hundred:	Hartismere
Union house:	Eye & Wortham
Deanery 2000:	Hartismere

7 miles NW of Eye between Botesdale & South Lopham. From the A143 turn onto B1113 into Redgrave, then right, into Churchway.
O.S. grid ref: TM 057782
Post Code: IP22 1RL

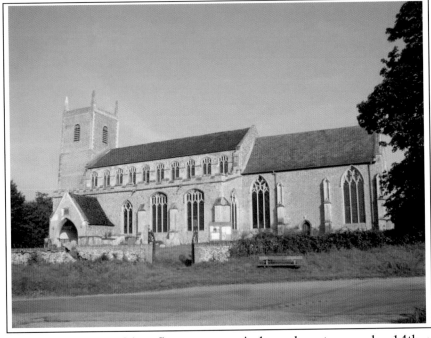

A lovely church with a fine twenty-window clerestory and a 14th c. porch. The buttresses on the chancel have empty niches. Inside, the church is spacious, and concerts and other functions are held here. The fabric is now maintained by The Churches Conservation Trust but the parish is responsible for improvements. The roof of the nave has hammerbeam and tiebeam with arch-bracing and queen posts. Morning is the best time to view the east window. The 14th c. font is nicely decorated and has faces round the corbel of the bowl. There is an old four-wheel bier on display. In the north aisle is a superb monument with life-size effigies of Sir Nicholas and Anne Bacon (1616). Anne's mother is remembered in brass in the chancel. There is a similar monument in the chancel to John Holt (1642).

REDLINGFIELD

Dedication:	St Andrew
No of Bells:	1
Deanery 1836:	Hartismere
Hundred:	Hartismere
Union house:	Eye & Wortham
Deanery 2000:	Hoxne

3 miles SE of Eye between Stradbroke & Thorndon. From B1117 W of Horham turn west into Low Road & follow 1 mile through village.
O.S. grid ref: TM 186707
Post Code: IP23 7QY

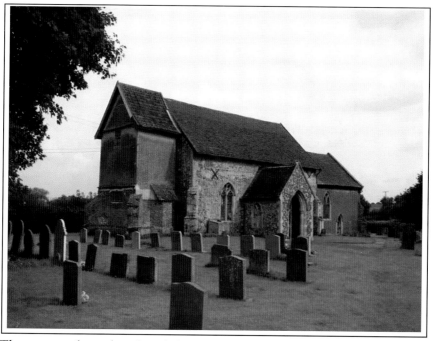

The approach to the church is no more than a hole in the hedge, just past the road-sign 'REDLINGFIELD' and before the Hall entrance. Parking on the road is quite risky. On the chancel wall is a monument to John Garneys, Gent of Kenton (1697). Inside the porch are stocks made for two, just in case the children are a problem. The building appears much older than its years, the chancel being 19th c. The tower has lost its top, and temporary repairs are here for the duration. There are signs of scratch dials on the south door. The font is the typical East Anglian type and badly mutilated, the cover is a simple cone with a cross on top. The only piscina is in the south wall of the nave. The Royal Arms are of George IIII *(sic)* and probably originally those of George III. Curiosity value only, I'm afraid.

RICKINGHALL INFERIOR

Dedication:	St Mary
No of Bells:	3
Deanery 1836:	Blackbourn
Hundred:	Blackbourn
Union house:	Onehouse
Deanery 2000:	Hartismere

7 miles W of Eye between Diss & Ixworth. Turn north off the A143 to Rickinghall. The church is beside the road and easy to find.

O.S. grid ref: TM 038751

Post Code: IP22 1HD

An unusual looking church, the huge porch seems disproportionately large. The tower was here in the 12th c., before the church was built, although the octagonal top is a 15th c. addition. The porch, which has a chamber above, and the nave are both 14th c., although the roof of the latter is a 16th c. hammerbeam with arch-bracing and collar. The south aisle and pier arcade are especially attractive, reflecting the fine workmanship on the exterior with the lovely pinnacled buttresses. There are restored 14th c. piscinas in both south aisle and chancel with dropped-sill sedilia. The octagonal font was never completely finished as one side is absolutely blank. Probably awaiting a benefactor! The reredos behind the holy table is made up from what appears to be the old rood screen.

RICKINGHALL SUPERIOR

Dedication:	St Mary
No of Bells:	6
Deanery 1836:	Hartismere
Hundred:	Hartismere
Union house:	Eye & Wortham
Deanery 2000:	Hartismere

7 miles W of Eye between Diss & Ixworth. Turn south off the A143 onto the B1113, Finningham Road. The church is directly on right.
O.S. grid ref: TM 040746
Post Code: IP22 1EH

This church is maintained by the Churches Conservation Trust and is no longer in regular use as a place of worship. The priests door in the chancel wall has a fine ogee arch and decorative hood-mould. A good example of flushwork can be seen around the parapet of the tower. Above the outer doorway of the porch are crowned 'M's of the BVM. This and other monograms are all of a very high quality. The church dates back to about the 14th c. but rebuilding of the nave took place in the 15th c. The piscina and neighbouring sedilia are both contemporary with the building. From behind the pulpit the rood loft stairs rise to an opening to nowhere. The octagonal pulpit bears blank shields, and behind it stands an old chest. The hand bier is similar to that at Rickinghall Inferior (p 172) and is dated 1763.

RISBY

Dedication: St Giles
No of Bells: 3
Deanery 1836: Thingoe
Hundred: Thingoe
Union house: Bury St Edmunds
Deanery 2000: Thingoe

4 miles NW of Bury St Eds. between Newmarket & Bury. Turn off the A14, 1 mile west of Bury St Eds. at Saxham Business Park.

O.S. grid ref: TL 802663
Post Code: IP28 6RQ

The church is in School Road, just east of the village centre. This is another of our Norman round tower churches. The nave and chancel are under one complete barn-type roof, indistinguishable from the outside. Inside the church the Norman chancel arch and piers are also original. On either side of the arch are a pair of canopied niches with cusped heads adorned with crockets. The 15th c. octagonal font has evangelistic carvings on the bowl, while the shaft has figures and tracery. The screen, which dates from the 15th c., had been modified over the years and was properly restored in 1966. Wall paintings dating back to the 14th c. are worth coming here to see, even if nothing else takes your interest and although feint are quite different from the norm. Some of the window glass is as early as 13th c..

RISHANGLES

Dedication:	St Margaret
No of Bells:	3 now removed
Deanery 1836:	Hartismere
Hundred:	Hartismere
Union house:	Eye & Wortham
Deanery 2000:	Hartismere

4 miles S of Eye between Eye & Debenham on the B1077. Once in the village the church is a few yards from the 'Y' junction.
O.S. grid ref: TM 160686
Post Code: IP23 7LB

This church was made redundant in 1971. It is now a private house. A public footpath passes close by but viewing inside is not possible. I can only refer to the work of others in telling you what this church once contained. I can confirm that very little has changed structurally on the outside, if you discount the fire escape coming down the 12th c. tower which is situated south of the nave. The south doorway through the tower still has all its Norman ornamentation. The north door is also Norman. Slit windows are further evidence of Norman builders if any were needed. The font was interesting but its age was in doubt. Without the foresight to domesticise this church it would probably be ruinous. It is one of several churches in Suffolk which have been saved by being turned into a dwelling house.

ROUGHAM

		4 miles SE of Bury St Eds.
Dedication:	St Mary	between Bury & Woolpit.
No of Bells:	5	South of the A14. The
Deanery 1836:	Thedwastre	church is about ½ mile
Hundred:	Thedwastre	north of the village.
Union house:	Bury St Edmunds	O.S. grid ref: TL 912625
Deanery 2000:	Lavenham	Post Code: IP30 9JJ

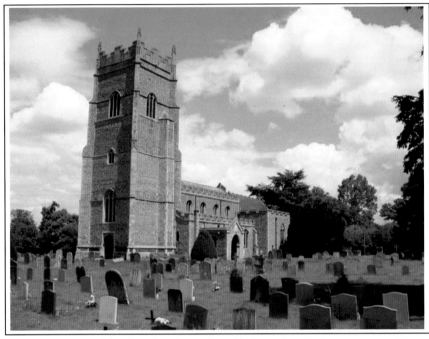

On seeing the this for the first time I thought, 'What a magnificent church!' There are probably 13th c. intramural burials here, as can be seen from the arches in the aisle wall just east of the 14th c. porch. There are inscriptions on the north aisle buttresses dated 1514, and on the porch roof dated 1632. Around the battlements of the tower there are more, asking for prayers for benefactors. The nave has a superb hammerbeam roof, the hammers of which are decapitated recumbent figures. The wall-posts have niches which are canopied and contain figures and the detail is striking. The attractive 14th c. piscina and sedilia have matching octagonal supports and cusped arches, whereas the 14th c. font is plain. Some benches, most of which have tracery on the backs are 15th c. and there are some nice poppyheads.

RUSHBROOK   *****
Dedication: St Nicholas
No of Bells: 3
Deanery 1836:   Thedwastre
Hundred: Thedwastre
Union house: Bury St Edmunds
Deanery 2000:   Lavenham

3 miles SE of Bury St Eds.
between Gt. Welnetham &
Rougham. Turn E off A134
opposite Nowton Park and
follow 2 m. into to Rushbrook
O.S. grid ref: TL 893615
Post Code: IP30 9HY

From the outside, except for the unusual crow step gable on the nave, this could be any 14th c. church. Inside, however, the feeling and the layout is different from any other church I know. I will start with the ordinary. The nave has an arch-braced roof. Everything else is different. The benches face north-south instead of east. The font is constructed of wood. The 16th c. roof trusses of the south aisle have a battlemented moulding and are painstakingly carved. Standing on a beam, where the rood loft should be, are the unique Royal Arms of Henry VIII. Incorporated into the reredos is a piscina. A monument to Thomas Jermyn (1692) age 15 has a much older reclining figure. There is a proliferation of monuments to Jermyns, Rushbrokes and Davers, mostly 17th c. If you like 'different', you'll like this.

SANTON DOWNHAM

Dedication:	St Mary	
No of Bells:	1	
Deanery 1836:	Fordham	
Hundred:	Lackford	
Union house:	Thetford	
Deanery 2000:	Mildenhall	

4 miles NW of Thetford between Thetford & Brandon. Turn north off the B1107 to Santon Downham. The church is beside the road.
O.S. grid ref: TL 816876
Post Code: IP27 0TQ

This little Saxon-Norman church looks as fresh as a daisy from the outside and lacks any buttressing. The Victorians, whom I often criticise for their 'over-restoration', have sympathetically preserved this church. The oldest part is the priest's doorway on the south side, circa 1170. Both north and south doorways have Norman candy-twist engaged columns, but dated a little later. The former has a depressed arch and a niche above. There are three Norman lancet windows with wide splays inside. The youngest part is the tower which is 15th c. and built in three stages. In the nave, on the wall of the tower are two memorials, one being to Col. Cadogan (1813). In the churchyard a headstone to John Gore has Masonic symbols and near the tower is the base of an old cross recovered from the woods nearby.

SAPISTON

Dedication:	St Andrew
No of Bells:	4
Deanery 1836:	Blackbourn
Hundred:	Blackbourn
Union house:	Thetford
Deanery 2000:	Ixworth

8 miles NE of Bury St Eds. between Ixworth & Thetford. From Honington on Bardwell Road, turn south opposite Old School House and follow lane.
O.S. grid ref: TL 920742
Post Code: IP31 1SA

This is yet another of the churches maintained by The Churches Conservation Trust. You will notice the porch is in need of structural support and is held together with iron braces. The beautiful Norman doorway it protects has the most unusual arch decoration I have seen in any small church. There are two octagonal engaged columns with cushion caps, each with a scratch dial. The arch has two orders of what I can only describe as 'tongue' decoration. Inside the doorway is a stoup which has been scooped out of the wall. The piscina in the chancel wall is 14th c. and has an unusually cusped arch. The undecorated octagonal font bowl has a cover 400 years its junior. Most of the nave roof has been renewed recently and only a few of the braced arch timbers remain, resting on hammerbeams.

SEMER

Dedication: All Saints
No of Bells: 3
Deanery 1836:   Sudbury
Hundred: Cosford
Union house: Semer
Deanery 2000:   Hadleigh

3 miles NW of Hadleigh between Hadleigh & Chelsworth. Turn off the B1115 south of Semer Bridge, drive across the meadow.
O.S. grid ref: TL 998467
Post Code: IP7 6JB

This church is tucked away almost out of sight and secluded. There is just a car-size gap in the hedge. It has been over-restored and some of the belfry sound holes are blocked with brickwork, marring the appearance. The porch is 15th c. but that too has been restored. The 14th c. font is a bulky item with the shaft only a few inches narrower than the bowl; which was square and has been crudely modified to octagonal, the cover is Stuart. The roof of the chancel and the screen are comparatively recent. Directly behind the pulpit is the organ. There are a few pieces of woodwork that are well carved and a couple of wall plaques in memory of Sarah Cooke (1752), wife of the vicar. There is another in black marble dated 1563. The corbels are different from the norm, having bulls with wings as well as angels.

SHELLAND

Dedication: King Charles the Martyr
No of Bells: 1
Deanery 1836:   Stow
Hundred: Stow
Union house: Onehouse
Deanery 2000:   Stowmarket

3 miles NW of Stowmarket
between Stowmarket &
Woolpit. From the A14 take
exit to Harleston. Bear right
after Harleston Hall for ½ m.
O.S. grid ref: TM 003602
Post Code: IP14 3DE

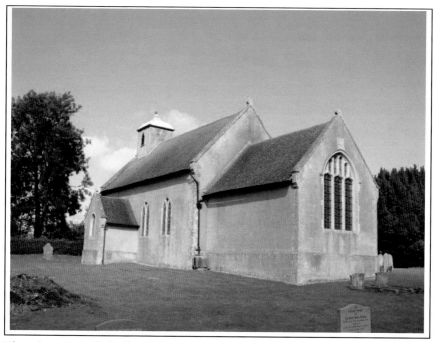

The church and dedication are unusual in being a donative, that is to say built and donated by the landowner, and one of only five churches in the country with a dedication to King Charles the Martyr. It was built in 1767 on the site of an earlier church about which we know very little. The outside is very plain and is cement-rendered. There is no tower but a small bellcote sits on the western end of the nave roof. The octagonal font is 14th c. and is from the earlier church. A three-decker pulpit, font cover and box pews are all of the same date. The moulded Royal Arms of Queen Victoria hang on the pink emulsioned wall of the nave. The chancel is a pastel green. It would be interesting to know what Dowsing's men would have made of the wall colourings in this lovely little church.

SHIMPLING

		7 miles S of Bury St Eds.
Dedication:	St George	between Long Melford &
No of Bells:	5	Bradfield. Turn off the
Deanery 1836:	Sudbury	A134 2 m north of Long
Hundred:	Babergh	Melford at Bridge Street.
Union house:	Sudbury	O.S. grid ref: TL 859513
Deanery 2000:	Sudbury	Post Code: IP29 4HF

Do not confuse Shimpling with Shimpling Street, they are over a mile apart. Originally the parish was called Shimplingthorne, and part of it still is. Situated in the village centre, just off the three-crossways, the churchyard contains the mausoleum of the Halifax family of Chadacre Hall. The lovely octagonal font is the only object of real interest here. It is late 14th c. with an uncommon shape and design. Eight clustered columns support the shallow carved bowl on an octagonal plinth. The panelled pulpit is square and has some carving in the form of cusped arches and religious symbols. There are wall monuments to members of the Halifax family, one of which set into the wall is particularly pleasing. It is of Thomas Halifax, and has carved angels kneeling and praying over a casket.

SOMERTON

Dedication:	All Saints	
No of Bells:	2	
Deanery 1836:	Sudbury	
Hundred:	Babergh	
Union house:	Sudbury	
Deanery 2000:	Sudbury	

8 miles NW of Sudbury between Hawkedon & Hartest. From the road between the above, turn north at Somerton Hall. O.S. grid ref: TL 810530 Post Code: IP29 4ND

From the road this church seems to have two aisles. It does not. What it is, is a chapel-cum-storeroom, and it houses the bulk of the organ. The Arms of George III hang on the wall. Before you enter, look to the west end of this chapel and you will notice part of a sepulchral slab built into the lower part of the wall. As you enter the porch you are confronted by a plain 12th c. Norman doorway into the nave. The font is 16th c. and not very interesting. All the shields round the bowl are blank. Both pulpit and holy table are Stuart. There is no chancel arch, just a variation in the wall alignment. The arcade between the 'chapel' and the sanctuary is 13th c. and there is an unusual pillared squint a little further east. The Rev. John Maddy (1855) is buried here, Canon of Ely and Chaplain in Ordinary to Queen Victoria.

STANNINGFIELD

Dedication:	St Nicholas	
No of Bells:	1	
Deanery 1836:	Clare	
Hundred:	Thedwastre	
Union house:	Bury St Edmunds	
Deanery 2000:	Thingoe	

6 miles S of Bury St Eds. between Bury & Long Melford. Turn off the A134 into Chapel Road, left at Hoggard's Green & follow.
O.S. grid ref: TL 877563
Post Code: IP29 4RB

A sad-looking church, with the top portion of the tower missing and a low pyramidal cap keeping out the rain. The doorways are Norman, the south protected by an ancient wooden porch. In the nave is a photograph of the church complete with the tower as it was. Only one small bell remains. Three clappers from the old bells hang in the base of the tower. Arcading and shields decorate the simple font. In the chancel the windows have unusual tracery which dates from the 14th c. and beneath is a blocked quatrefoil opening. Built into the north wall of the sanctuary is a canopied Easter sepulchre formed from an altar tomb bearing the arms of the Rokewood family. Above the chancel arch is a doom painting which carries much detail. It is a good idea to take your binoculars for a closer view.

STANSFIELD

Dedication:	All Saints
No of Bells:	5
Deanery 1836:	Clare
Hundred:	Risbridge
Union house:	Haverhill
Deanery 2000:	Clare

9 miles SW of Bury St Eds. between Stradishall & Boxford. Between Denston & Hawkedon turn south. Church within 200 yards.
O.S. grid ref: TL 783525
Post Code: CO10 8LU

Stansfield church is perched on the brow of a hill heading down into the village below. The road is not best suited to park a car. It is quite an impressive church for a small parish and has a scratch dial on a buttress. It doesn't have a clerestory and the windows of the embattled south aisle are not large enough to allow enough light into the 14th c. nave. This unfortunately makes it quite a dark church, especially on a dull day. The font is of two distinct parts; the roughly carved bowl is 16th c. The four clusters of three columns which support it look like new. Between the chancel and the chapel is a 13th c. arcade of two arches. Nearby is a coeval pillared squint. In the chancel there is an iron-bound chest, above which is the piscina. A Stuart pulpit with steps leading up to it stands on a stumpy pillar.

STANSTEAD
Dedication: St James
No of Bells: 1
Deanery 1836:   Sudbury
Hundred: Babergh
Union house: Sudbury
Deanery 2000:   Sudbury

6 miles NW of Sudbury
between Long Melford &
Boxted. Turn north off the
B1066 near The Old Forge
into village centre.
O.S. grid ref: TL 843493
Post Code: CO10 9AT

A pleasant enough little church, set back off the road at the back of the green behind a lychgate that wouldn't keep the rain off in a light shower. The gable cross leans against the south chancel wall, and the 14th c. tower has been declared unsafe (2008). At the north east corner of the chancel there are bricks with initials and dates scratched into them, probably benefactors for the repairs. One is marked 'JB 1793' others are dated 1811. I could find no additional information. The crenulated porch has crocketted pinnacles and a stoup. The font has simple quatrefoil decoration. Both nave and chancel roofs are arch-braced tie-beam construction. Queen Anne's Arms are a very good example of the kind. Beneath the tower arch sits one of the redundant bells. Once there were six, now only one remains.

STANTON

Dedication: All Saints
No of Bells: 4
Deanery 1836: Blackbourn
Hundred: Blackbourn
Union house: Bury St Edmunds
Deanery 2000: Ixworth

9 miles NE of Bury St Eds.
between The Rickinghalls
& Ixworth. Turn south off
the A143 and follow road to
village centre.
O.S. grid ref: TL 965734
Post Code: IP31 2DB

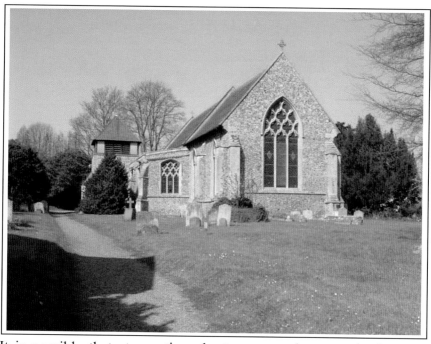

It is possible that at one time the tower stood separately from the church and was only linked in the 14th c. when the south aisle was built. Until 1906 the tower stood 70 feet high, but it collapsed and was never rebuilt. Instead, a belfry was added to the consolidated remains of the tower. Beneath the tower is the entrance to the nave. You are greeted by the sight of the plain 13th c. octagonal font standing on a plinth. It has a central shaft surrounded by eight small columns. The pulpit has a similar appearance. In the wall of the south aisle is a lovely 14th c. crocketted piscina which also opens into the window reveal. In the chancel is another, less elaborate, adjacent to a three-seater sedilia. A tomb recess in the south aisle has carvings worthy of close examination. Plenty of interest for the visitor here.

STANTON

Dedication:	St John	
No of Bells:	4 now removed	
Deanery 1836:	Blackbourn	
Hundred:	Blackbourn	
Union house:	Bury St Edmunds	
Deanery 2000:	Ixworth	

9 miles NE of Bury St Eds. between The Rickinghalls and Ixworth. Turn <u>north</u> off the A143 into Bardwell Rd and stop. Church on right.
O.S. grid ref: TL 962737
Post Code: IP31 2EA

The church of St. John is derelict and has been for over a century. It is now cared for and maintained by the Churches Conservation Trust. The tower is still intact and stands at the same height Stanton All Saints once was (see p. 187). Everything has been removed from the building, including the roofs of the nave and chancel. The sanctus bell window in the east wall of the tower can be clearly seen. The Royal Arms of George III, as well as other bits and pieces, were removed to All Saints. Because the church is built directly against the western boundary, it required an archway to be built beneath the tower to allow processions to circumnavigate the church without having to leave consecrated ground. This feature can also be seen at Combs (see p. 46).

STOKE ASH

Dedication:	All Saints
No of Bells:	5
Deanery 1836:	Hartismere
Hundred:	Hartismere
Union house:	Eye & Wortham
Deanery 2000:	Hartismere

3 miles SSW of Eye between Diss & The Stonhams. Stoke Ash is clearly signed east off the A140. The church is near Hall Farm.

O.S. grid ref: TM 115704

Post Code: IP23 7ET

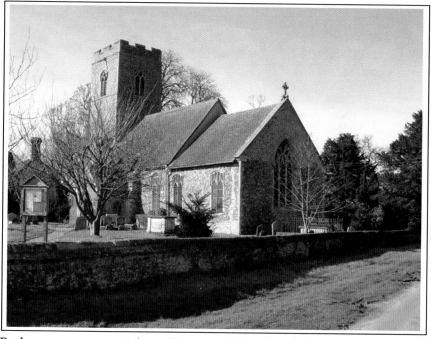

Perhaps you may catch a glimpse of this church from the A140. But it is well worth a closer look. It is usually locked but a keyholder is not too far away. The Tudor red-brick porch has an empty niche above the doorway. Inside there is a small stoup. The doorway is Norman but plain and uninteresting, likewise the north doorway. The irregular octagonal font is in the same category, but nearby is the upper part of one of the bells which cracked. The inscription is still quite clear. Information boards explain more. Near the Stuart pulpit the old rood loft stairs are still open, the steps starting in the window recess. The piscina and sedilia in the chancel are very plain. Two marble plaques to Frances (1718) and Mary (1719) Bedingfelde hang on the wall. The reredos is a memorial to Joseph Moss (1917).

STOKE BY CLARE

Dedication:	St John the Baptist
No of Bells:	6 + 1 clock bell
Deanery 1836:	Clare
Hundred:	Risbridge
Union house:	Haverhill
Deanery 2000:	Clare

5 miles SE of Haverhill between Haverhill & Clare. Church is beside the A1092 near the grassed area on a bend.

O.S. grid ref: TL 741433

Post Code: CO10 8JA

Under the window of one of the cottages near the church is what I believe is the base of an old cross. The 14th c. tower dominates the church building. Round the back is a door to the stairs leading upwards. The outward appearance of this low squat-looking church is deceptive. Inside, it is nothing of the sort. It is tall with lofty arches and plenty of light from the clerestory. The octagonal font is nothing out of the ordinary, it is the small 15th c. pulpit that is exceptional. The tracery is quite different from any other and is arguably the finest in the county. A glimpse behind the organ pipes will reveal a painting of The Doom, and although not as spectacular as that at Wenhaston (E. Sfk. p. 275) it is still in reasonable condition. There is a fine parish chest and some of the carved bench ends are quite elaborate.

STOKE BY NAYLAND

Dedication:	St Mary
No of Bells:	6 + 1 clock bell
Deanery 1836:	Sudbury
Hundred:	Babergh
Union house:	Sudbury
Deanery 2000:	Hadleigh

8 miles SE of Sudbury between Nayland & Polstead. Either the B1068 or the B1087 to the church. Easily found by virtue of the tower. O.S. grid ref: TL 986362 Post Code: CO6 4QU

The 120-feet-tall 15th c. tower can be seen from many miles away, and is easily recognisable by its pinnacles. The west tower doorway has arms of the Tendring and Howard families. The entrance. however, is through the south porch. On the door is fine tracery and carving which must have looked wonderful when it was new. Over the porch is a chamber. Pier arcades line the nave with its splendid tie beams supported on corbels, each carved with a face. The 15th c. font which stands on a stepped plinth is carved with evangelistic scenes and has angels round the corbel of the bowl. 14th c. misericordes and some benches are worth a close look. There is a very fine monument with an effigy of Katherine Howard (1452). Another even earlier monument is to Sir William Tendring (1408).

STOWLANGTOFT

Dedication:	St George
No of Bells:	4
Deanery 1836:	Blackbourn
Hundred:	Blackbourn
Union house:	Onehouse
Deanery 2000:	Ixworth

7 miles NE of Bury St Eds. between Ixworth & Badwell Ash. From the A1088 turn east, 2 m south of Ixworth or 4 m north of Elmswell. O.S. grid ref: TL 957682 Post Code: IP31 3JR

Here, behind the wall of flint, integrated with window tracery and other ecclesiastical stonework, is a fine late 14th c. church you will love to visit and re-visit. There is much to see here, from the beautiful chequer-work on the porch to the Flemish wall panelling, famous for having part of it stolen and later recovered. Above the chancel arch can be seen what remains of the canopy of honour. The wall painting of St Christopher is hardly discernable. Standing on a plinth at the west end of the nave is the early 14th c. octagonal font with carved bowl and fluted shaft. The 15th c. benches have wonderful carvings of real and imaginary creatures. Similarly the superb misericordes have mermaids and dragons with armrests of old men with long beards. The parish chest is enormous.

STOWMARKET

Dedication: Sts Peter & Mary
No of Bells: 8
Deanery 1836: Stow
Hundred: Stow
Union house: Onehouse
Deanery 2000: Stowmarket

12 miles NW of Ipswich between Bury St Edmunds & Ipswich. In Station Road West on the B1115 near the junction of the A1308.
O.S. grid ref: TM 049586
Post Code: IP14 1EF

There is no other spire in the county which is anything like this one, erected in 1994 with a viewing platform and cross keys emblem. Before the 15th c. it was a much smaller church, and what is now the north aisle may well have been the nave. The present nave and south aisle were constructed with the wealth of the wool trade when the river was navigable to Ipswich. Signs of anything earlier than Victorian were largely erased in the 19th c. although there is a 13th c. coped sepulchral slab in the south aisle. The north aisle contains many monuments as well as a chapel to the Tyrell family. There is a 14th c. canopy tomb, said to be that of an abbot. Some grotesques are carved into arm rests of the bench ends. Headstones have been moved to give the graveyard the appearance of a park.

STOWUPLAND

Dedication:	Holy Trinity	
No of Bells:	1	
Deanery 1836:	Stow	
Hundred:	Stow	
Union house:	Onehouse	
Deanery 2000:	Stowmarket	

2 miles NE of Stowmarket between Little Stonham and Stowmarket. On the A1120 at the bottom of the hill near the school.

O.S. grid ref: TM 071600

Post Code: IP14 4BQ

Stowupland church is Victorian, built in 1843 with white bricks. It has an elegant copper-clad broached spire. In the churchyard at a bend in the path there is a memorial with an unusual illustration of a serpent wrapped round a shillelagh drinking from the fountain of life. The rather plain font was rescued from Creeting All Saints which until 1800 stood in the same churchyard as Creeting St Mary (E. Suffolk. p. 70), about three miles away. Hanging at the west end is the cast iron Royal Arms of George IV. The woodwork of course is mostly Victorian and coeval with the church, but the 17th c. pulpit is beautifully carved with scenes from the early life of Jesus, including circumcision and presentation at the temple amongst others. It is of foreign origin, probably Flemish, so I was told.

STRADISHALL

Dedication:	St Margaret
No of Bells:	5
Deanery 1836:	Clare
Hundred:	Risbridge
Union house:	Haverhill
Deanery 2000:	Clare

6 miles NE of Haverhill between Haverhill and Bury St Edmunds. Turn off the A143 near the prison and follow the B1063 ½ mile. O.S. grid ref: TL 747525 Post Code: CB8 8YW

A few years ago there was a parishioner who used to care for the church and churchyard; he was church warden and keyholder. Now he rests in the sadly neglected graveyard he tended for all his adult life, and the church is miserably desolate. There are heaters inside, perhaps that is why the doors are locked! In a few years this church will be redundant. The octagonal font, seen through the window, is 15th c. with quatrefoil decoration. Some wall paintings are close to being destroyed by the green slime growing on the walls. There are a number of wall plaques to be seen. One is to William Rayner who was from Stradishall Place and died in 1845. His wife Frances is on his left. This could be a lovely church; instead it is just a shed for storing heaters! Such a shame.

STUSTON

Dedication:	All Saints	
No of Bells:	4	
Deanery 1836:	Hartismere	
Hundred:	Hartismere	
Union house:	Eye & Wortham	
Deanery 2000:	Hartismere	

3 miles N of Eye between Diss & Eye. From the A140 or A143 take the B1077 between the two. North into narrow lane, follow 300 yds. O.S. grid ref: TM 134778
Post Code: IP21 4AG

The round tower has a later octagonal belfry stage with a red brick parapet. Inside both the south and north porches is a stoup. H. Munro Cautley says there is nothing else of interest in this badly restored church. I agree that the octagonal font is very plain and without decoration, and that the wagon style of the nave roof is black and dismal. The woodwork is certainly very simple, even that of the pulpit. What H. forgot was the king-post roof in the chancel and the monument to Sir John Castleton (1727) and to Bridget his wife on the wall below. If you visit this church you will also notice the way the bricks in all the arches have been painted, red, black and yellow. Initially I was quite shocked at the bizarre appearance, but my eye soon became accustomed to the effect and it became quite pleasing.

SUDBURY

Dedication:	All Saints
No of Bells:	8 + 1 clock bell
Deanery 1836:	Sudbury
Hundred:	Sudbury
Union house:	Sudbury
Deanery 2000:	Sudbury

16 miles S of Bury St
Edmunds between
Newmarket & Colchester.
In Church Street just off the
A131 towards Bulmer Tye.
O.S. grid ref: TL 868409
Post Code: CO10 2BL

One of the three major churches in Sudbury which date from around the 15th c., just before the Tudors. It has a superb west tower with a stair turret rising above the double crenulated parapet. Just inside the south porch is a stoup. On entering the nave, the pier arcade is impressive, the roof has cambered tie beams and arch-braced principals above the lovely ten-light clerestory. There seems to be an abundance of fine tracery on the windows and doors, everywhere you look. The fine 15th c. pulpit stands on one spindly pillar, the coeval font bears even more tracery on the bowl and shaft. A few interesting carvings can be found on various benches. Painted on the wall of the Eden chapel is the 17th c. pedigree of the Eden and Waldegrave families. It has far more of interest than St Peter's on Market Hill.

SUDBURY

Dedication: St Gregory
No of Bells: 8
Deanery 1836: Sudbury
Hundred: Sudbury
Union house: Sudbury
Deanery 2000: Sudbury

16 miles S of Bury St
Edmunds between
Newmarket & Colchester.
On Gregory Street on the
way to Long Melford.
O.S. grid ref: TL 870414
Post Code: CO10 1AZ

A church, like the other two in Sudbury, built on the wealth created by the wool trade, and the most interesting of the three. The grand tower has a stair turret rising above the top of the parapet. Inside the porch is a stoup and the doors have traceried heads to the panels. In the expanse of the nave you are greeted by the 15th c. 12 feet high font cover about which, details are posted on the wall. The nave itself is not wide but the arcades are impressive. The roof is cambered tie beam construction with arch bracing. The misericordes are worthy of a close look as they are all different. Adjoining the porch is a chapel which has a table tomb and wall monument to Thomas Carter (1706). The most bizarre possession of the church is the skull of Simon of Sudbury, Archbishop of Canterbury, beheaded in 1381.

SUDBURY

Dedication:	St Peter	
No of Bells:	8	
Deanery 1836:	Sudbury	
Hundred:	Sudbury	
Union house:	Sudbury	
Deanery 2000:	Sudbury	

16 miles S of Bury St
Edmunds between
Newmarket & Colchester.
At the top of Market Hill in
the town centre.
O.S. grid ref: TL 874413
Post Code: CO10 2EA

The most prominent of Sudbury's three major churches, and the only one which is redundant as a church. Supported by the Churches Conservation Trust, it is preserved in the hope that one day it may again be used for worship. It is usually locked but the nearby tourist office will direct you to the key. Entry is through the west door of the tower. Inside you will find a large empty space surrounded by large empty walls apart from publicity for the CCT. Behind curtains in what was a chapel are piles of chairs waiting to be set out for an audience. The 15th c. octagonal font has a nice conical cover. Below the sanctuary is a sacristy, accessible through a sunken doorway. There are two piscina, one in the nave the other adjacent to panel-lined sedilia in the chancel.

THELNETHAM

Dedication: St Nicholas
No of Bells: 5
Deanery 1836: Blackbourn
Hundred: Blackbourn
Union house: Thetford
Deanery 2000: Ixworth

9 miles E of Thetford between Hopton St Mary & Redgrave. At the junction of Hopton Road and Church Lane in the village centre.
O.S. grid ref: TM 018783
Post Code: IP22 1JZ

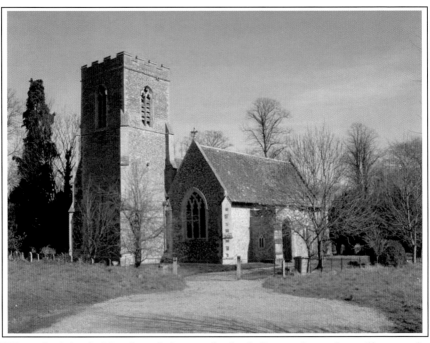

When I visited this church it was locked. I was forced to glimpse the 17th c. Bockenham wall monument through the window of the nave. Fortunately the glass was clear. In fact the only thing of value in the church are the windows. The 14th c. font is plain, the piscina, although quite elaborate, has been restored and is of no interest. Perhaps it is the roof of the chancel that might get pinched! It is of locally grown sweet chestnut. Perhaps, then, the stone mensas weighing about half a ton each are in danger of being stolen! Even the crosses thereon have been re-cut and are not original. Maybe the relief carving on the wall of the north wall of the nave is under threat! So why Thelnetham P.C.C., is the church kept locked? Are you afraid someone is going to pinch the bells?

THORNDON

Dedication: All Saints
No of Bells: 6
Deanery 1836:   Hartismere
Hundred: Hartismere
Union house: Eye & Wortham
Deanery 2000:   Hartismere

3 miles S of Eye between Eye & Debenham. Either from the B1077 or the A140 to Thorndon. The church is set back 100 yds off the road. O.S. grid ref: TM 142696
Post Code: IP23 7JR

The nave was built in the 13th c. and the tower was added a century later for the purpose of combining a porch with somewhere to hang the bells. A stoup with a cusped arch and hood sits in the angle of a buttress near the door. On the south wall is what appears to be a semi intramural burial, with a low arch and stone coffin lid behind a table tomb. At the west end the church is bang up to date, with toilets and a small kitchen being fitted when I called. The octagonal font is typical 15th c. East Anglian style and virtually unmarked. Also in pristine condition is the lovely cusped piscina, beside which is a sedilia into which has been set the altar rail. I was pleased to see the rood stairs open from bottom to top. Nearby is the Stuart pulpit. The corbels supporting the roof are unusually large angels.

THORNHAM MAGNA

Dedication:	St Mary
No of Bells:	5
Deanery 1836:	Hartismere
Hundred:	Hartismere
Union house:	Eye & Wortham
Deanery 2000:	Hartismere

3 miles SW of Eye between Eye & Finningham. From the village centre go north along The Street, past the road junction on the left.
O.S. grid ref: TM 104714
Post Code: IP23 8HA

Standing close to the entrance of Thornham Park, a sense of tranquillity permeates this pleasant typical East Anglian churchyard. Trimmed Irish yews stand like sentinels among the headstones. Entry into the 15th c. nave is through the south porch with its flint and stone flushwork which incorporates three niches. Inside, the Victorian nave roof is a single hammerbeam type. Scattered around the walls are many hatchments of the Henniker family. The church itself has been very much restored and very little of historical or architectural interest remains. However the church does have its treasures. A great 19th c. marble monument to Lord John and Lady Emily Henniker depicts two women supporting an urn bearing the faces of the couple. Other monuments adorn the walls.

THORNHAM PARVA

Dedication:	St Mary
No of Bells:	1
Deanery 1836:	Hartismere
Hundred:	Hartismere
Union house:	Eye & Wortham
Deanery 2000:	Hartismere

2 miles SW of Eye between Eye & Finningham. Follow the road north from Thornham Magna and turn right <u>after</u> Church Lane.
O.S. grid ref: TM 109726
Post Code: IP23 8EY

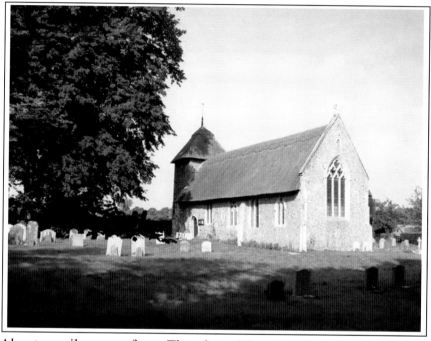

About a mile away from Thornham Magna and set back from the road behind trees the church is almost hidden from view. It is older in its origins than the aforementioned: still thatched, including the little pyramidal cap atop the tower. Note that the flint stones that create the walls are laid in courses. Two Norman doorways, north and south. and a slit window post-date the beginnings of this church. although there is little evidence of Saxon work today. Inside the nave the walls are covered in 14th c. early mediaeval paintings. Some consecration crosses seem to be coeval. The octagonal font, standing on an octagonal shaft, has traceried panels, and an iron-bound ark chest is also of the same period. The western gallery is still useable. Behind the altar is a remarkable retable dating from around 1300.

THORPE MORIEUX

Dedication:	St Mary	
No of Bells:	3	
Deanery 1836:	Sudbury	
Hundred:	Cosford	
Union house:	Semer	
Deanery 2000:	Lavenham	

9 miles SE of Bury St Eds. between Brettenham & Cockfield. From Brettenham, south to Buckingham school gates, follow signpost ¾ mile.
O.S. grid ref: TL 943533
Post Code: IP30 0NW

The Norman connection is in the name of the parish but the church is basically 14th c. The tower was added later and is 15th c. Next to the lovely 400 year-old porch is an unusual triangular-shaped buttress. Another variation of this can be found along the walls of the chancel. Oldest of all is the 13th c. square font, which has nice examples of early scratched chevrons and linear designs. It stands on its original shaft and four columns. On the wall below the Roll of Honour, is a beautiful image bracket, discovered hidden in the 14th c. nave piscina during restoration. In the chancel is an older piscina by 100 years. There are two memorials, one to Rev. John Fiske (1761) and his wife Elizabeth (1749), who was descended from the Gosnold family. A second is to their daughter Sarah, and John Harrison her husband.

THRANDESTON

Dedication: St Margaret
No of Bells: 5
Deanery 1836: Hartismere
Hundred: Hartismere
Union house: Eye & Wortham
Deanery 2000: Hartismere

3 miles NW of Eye between Scole & Mellis. Heading north on the A140 turn left in the 40 mph limit then bear left and follow signs. O.S. grid ref: TM 116764
Post Code: IP21 4BX

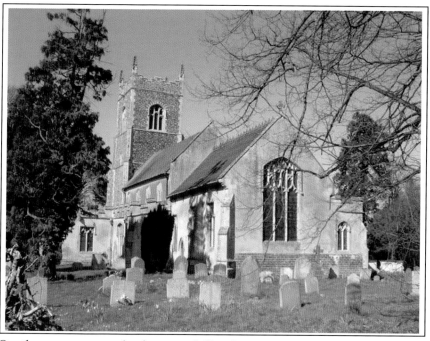

On the west tower the layers of flint between the quoins shows how much upward progress was made each year by the builders. At the top the embattled parapet has delicately crocketted pinnacles at each corner. There is a scratch dial on one of the buttresses. The clerestory windows light up the nave roof, around the cornice of which are painted shields and foliar designs. A typical East Anglian font stands on a plinth the same size as the base. The pulpit is octagonal with open traceried panels. A Peter's Pence box, of no great age, stands near the door on a pillar. There is some beautifully carved traceried panelling to admire on the 15th c. stalls and figures of St Peter and St John at the entrance. Above the chancel arch hang the Royal Arms of Queen Victoria.

THURSTON

Dedication:	St Peter	
No of Bells:	5	
Deanery 1836:	Thedwastre	
Hundred:	Thedwastre	
Union house:	Onehouse	
Deanery 2000:	Ixworth	

4 miles E of Bury St Edmunds between Bury & Stowmarket. Turn off A14 onto Thurston Road and take second right, then left and under bridge.
O.S. grid ref: TL 929652
Post Code: IP31 3RU

This church had to be almost entirely rebuilt. As can be seen from the picture and photograph in the nave, the 14th c. tower collapsed in 1860 taking with it most of the nave. As can be seen from one of the paintings the roof was once arch-braced with king-posts. The chancel is much as it always was, however with two piscinas, each unusually with their credence shelf. Adjacent is a three-level sedilia with cusped arches and carved spandrels. One or two poppyheads might catch your eye, the octagonal pulpit certainly will, beautifully carved with saints within cusped arches in the facets. High on the wall is a monument to William Smith and eleven members of his family. There are some 15th c. benches with traceried backs and ends but the majority of the woodwork is Victorian, including the rood screen.

THWAITE

Dedication:	St George	
No of Bells:	1	
Deanery 1836:	Hartismere	
Hundred:	Hartismere	
Union house:	Eye & Wortham	
Deanery 2000:	Hartismere	

5 miles S of Eye between Wickham Skeith & Thorndon. Turn west off the A140 at The Buck PH. Follow for 275 yards.
O.S. grid ref: TM 113681
Post Code: IP23 7EE

When I visited this church it had just become redundant. The P.C.C. have plans to keep it in use for the benefit of the parish. I wish them luck. It has no tower. When it fell the stone and flint was used to build the schoolhouse (near the road) and the cottages to the east. A small bellcote with a single bell stands precariously at the west end of the nave roof. The porch has an arch-braced collar roof with heads on the lower end of the braces. The 14th c. octagonal font has an alternating arcade and quatrefoil design. Above, the nave roof is single hammerbeam and arched bracing. There is a real treasure here, namely the 15th c. pulpit, similar to the renowned Wycliffe pulpit at Lutterworth. The tracery is coarse but beautifully executed. It will probably be removed to a museum as the use of the building changes.

TIMWORTH

Dedication:	St Andrew
No of Bells:	3
Deanery 1836:	Thedwastre
Hundred:	Thedwastre
Union house:	Bury St Edmunds
Deanery 2000:	Thingoe

3 miles N of Bury St Eds.
between Great Barton &
Culford. From Fornham
follow A134 north towards
Thetford, turn right & follow.
O.S. grid ref: TL 860697
Post Code: IP31 1HY

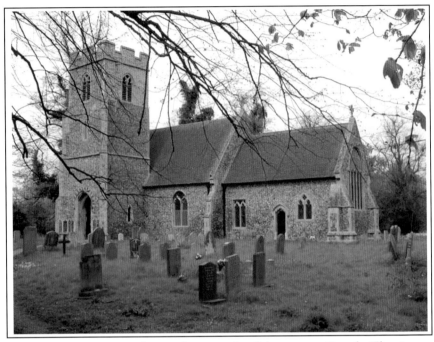

Turn down an unmade track opposite Livermere Road. The tower serves as a porch built onto the south of the nave, as opposed to the west. The porch is also the ringing chamber. On the tower there is what may be a transition between a scratch dial and sundial. It is purposely set to face due south and is at the height of the top of the arch, to the right. In 1865 the Rev. Benyon brought the very large 18th c. pulpit from St James at Bury St Edmunds. The panels on the facades of the pulpit are 16th c. There is nothing of real interest to the historian or architectural student here. The Victorians saw to that. I found it locked, and admittedly there is a keyholder, but there is no reason whatsoever why this church could not be left unlocked for the visitor or family history researcher. There's nothing left to steal.

TOSTOCK

Dedication:	St Andrew
No of Bells:	6
Deanery 1836:	Thedwastre
Hundred:	Thedwastre
Union house:	Onehouse
Deanery 2000:	Ixworth

6 miles E of Bury St Eds. between Thurston & Woolpit. Turn off the A14 at Woolpit/ Eriswell junction, take A1088 & turn left to Tostock.
O.S. grid ref: TL 960636
Post Code: IP30 9PQ

This is such a pretty little church, not from the road, but from the south. Entry is by the 15th c. south porch. The stoup has been filled in, and the unusual tracery in the window has been treated likewise. To the north is the 14th c. octagonal font with foliated facets to the bowl. To the east, a hoard of beasts and mythological creatures await your delight on the ends of the beautifully carved benches, the backs of which are also decoratively carved. The comparatively small 14th c. chancel has a wonderful double hammerbeam roof, so elaborate for such a small area. The nave roof too is double hammerbeam alternating with arch-braced principals. The span of the roof is an impressive 27 feet.   A rather plain piscina in the chancel seems inadequate somehow, when all else is so interesting.

TROSTON		5 miles NE of Bury St Eds.
Dedication:	St Mary	between Gt. Livermere &
No of Bells:	6	Honington. From Honington
Deanery 1836:	Blackbourn	turn SW to the village, then
Hundred:	Blackbourn	straight on, into Church Lane.
Union house:	Bury St Edmunds	O.S. grid ref: TL 900722
Deanery 2000:	Ixworth	Post Code: IP31 1EX

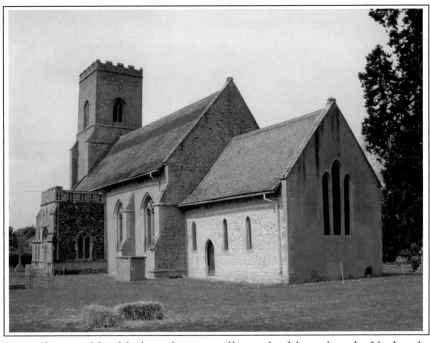

From the outside this is quite an ordinary looking church. Under the eaves of the nave are 17th c. springers (projections that support an internal arch) which are most uncommon. The porch has flushwork but post-dates the 14th c. nave by a century or two. Inside the nave you are greeted by an enormous wall painting on the left of the north door, of St George slaying the Dragon, and on the right St Christopher. A smaller George and Dragon is even earlier, probably coeval with the 13th c. chancel, in which there is a simple double piscina and adjacent sedilia. The screen which carries the rood, has been repainted fairly faithfully, although Cautley does not fully agree. The pulpit and reading desk are as one, of the Stuart period. The Royal Arms are of James I despite being over-painted 'G-R'.

TUDDENHAM ST MARY

Dedication:	St Mary
No of Bells:	5
Deanery 1836:	Fordham
Hundred:	Lackford
Union house:	Mildenhall
Deanery 2000:	Mildenhall

9 miles NW of Bury St Eds. between Cavenham & Barton Mills. Just south of the Barton Mills roundabout turn left and follow 2 miles. O.S. grid ref: TL 738713 Post Code: IP28 6SA

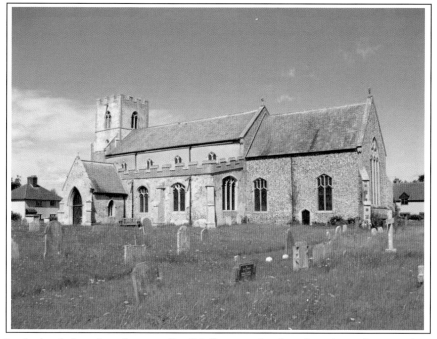

I admired the abundance of wild flowers in the churchyard more than the appearance of the church, I'm afraid. The fabric is crumbling and lacks the maintenance it deserves. It has stood here since the 14th c. and the clerestory was added a century later. Inside the nave is a lovely hammerbeam and arch-braced roof. The semi octagonal font is unusual in that it has a bevel round the top of the bowl and tapers towards the bottom. It stands on a square shaft with an engaged column at each corner. The rood loft stairs disappear into the chancel arch just behind the pulpit. Set into the north wall is an old tomb, probably later used as an Easter sepulchre. The church is large and empty and is devoid of character or interest. It was at one time a fine church, but alas, no more.

WALSHAM LE WILLOWS

Dedication:	St Mary
No of Bells:	6
Deanery 1836:	Blackbourn
Hundred:	Blackbourn
Union house:	Onehouse
Deanery 2000:	Ixworth

10 miles NE of Bury St Eds. between Finningham & Stanton. From the A143 turn south at Hepworth X-rds, and follow for 2½ miles. O.S. grid ref: TL 999711 Post Code: IP31 3AB

As you approach the church the 24-light clerestory is probably the thing which stands out most or perhaps the chequer-work on the 16th c. porch. The date 1541 is written on the inside wall. Inside the nave, the early 15th c. roof has braced tie-beams with arched braces and intermittent hammerbeams. Each beam and hammer has two rows of detailed decoration. The octagonal font is 14th c. with cusping round the bowl and shallow arcading on the shaft. Unexpectedly, the cusped piscina and sedilia are quite plain. Dating back to the 13th c. are the iron-clad parish chest and a sepulchral slab. An old 17th c. bier is used as a table for displaying leaflets. The rood screen has been re-painted in traditional colours. The 1883 reredos is a depiction of the Last Supper, by Tinworth , and is absolutely magnificent.

WANGFORD

Dedication:	St Denys
No of Bells:	1
Deanery 1836:	Fordham
Hundred:	Lackford
Union house:	Mildenhall
Deanery 2000:	Mildenhall

6 miles W of Thetford, Nfk between Eriswell & Brandon. Turn off the A1065 to Lakenheath and B1112 immediately left.
O.S. grid ref: TL 750835
Post Code: IP27 0SJ

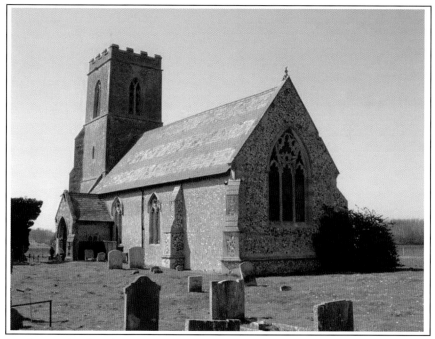

At the end of a dusty trackway is the church and its 14th c. tower. Both have stood up well over the centuries. The church has two Norman doorways with detached columns topped by cushion caps: the arches themselves are replacements. There is little left of the original church. The nave has been almost completely rebuilt although some parts of the old walls are incorporated in the new. In the 1970s the church was made redundant and is now in the hands of an American religious sect. With doors securely locked against all visitors, and windows blocked, there is no telling what goes on inside. There is no keyholder and you get the impression that you are very unwelcome here. Some day we shall, hopefully be able to have a look round the interior again.

WATTISFIELD

Dedication:	St Margaret
No of Bells:	5
Deanery 1836:	Blackbourn
Hundred:	Blackbourn
Union house:	Onehouse
Deanery 2000:	Ixworth

9 miles W of Eye between Diss & Ixworth. Once in Wattisfield on the A143 take the road south at the cross-roads near community centre.
O.S. grid ref: TM 010741
Post Code: IP22 1NS

One of the five bells is 16th c., cast in the 26th year of the reign of Elizabeth (1584). The church is 15th c. and has had noticeable restoration through the centuries. There are porches both north and south, the former being used as an entrance. It is a wooden structure that has served since the 16th c. The south porch is of stone and brick. Above the arch are the arms of the De la Poles and above those is sundial. Inside the nave stands the 15th c. octagonal font, the bowl is decorated with blank shields and the shaft traceried. The pyramidal font cover is 17th c. Stuart. Above, the roof is Victorian, scissor-braced style. The rood loft stairs are still open. In the chancel the piscina is of an unusual style and is flanked by the almost customary dropped-sill sedilia.

WATTISHAM

Dedication:	St Nicholas
No of Bells:	2
Deanery 1836:	Sudbury
Hundred:	Cosford
Union house:	Semer
Deanery 2000:	Hadleigh

5 miles SW of Stowmarket
between Stowmarket &
Lavenham. West of the
airfield, on the road to
Bildeston. Easy to miss!
O.S. grid ref: TM 009513
Post Code: IP7 7JU

A sad little church, secreted behind a hedge next to Wattisham Hall. Inside the porch, the south doorway is Norman, with a detached column either side. On the door there is a 14th c. ring handle and back-plate. Declared redundant in the 1970s, it is still in use as a venue for meetings and as a village hall. It is struggling to survive despite being funded by Heritage Lottery money. The octagonal font has unusual billeting around the top of the bowl. A dormer window in the north and south-facing roof of the chancel once shed light onto the rood. The roofs are simple arch-braced and have been plaster-boarded. Where the altar once stood is the bar, and the benches have been replaced by tables and chairs. A large ledger slab on the floor is to 17th c. knight, Sir William Blomfeild.

WEST ROW

		2½ miles E of Mildenhall
Dedication:	St Peter	between the Airbase &
No of Bells:	1	Freckenham, at the junction
Deanery 1836:	hamlet of Mildenhall	of Friday Street, Church
Hundred:	hamlet of Mildenhall	Road & Church Lane.
Union house:	hamlet of Mildenhall	O.S. grid ref: TL 674754
Deanery 2000:	Mildenhall	Post Code: IP28 8PF

Half-hidden by trees of various species this little church was built in 1850 as a school. It became a church in 1875 when West Row was declared a parish and no longer a hamlet of Mildenhall. New windows were put in, a porch and vestry were added, and the appearance of the whole building was changed. Inside the church the chancel arch is cusped, which appears most strange. The roof is supported with queen-posts. The furnishings, pews, pulpit and stalls, indeed everything in the church is contemporary it and purely functional. It is an honest building, and no attempt has been made to make it anything other than what it is. It sits in its own very neat and tidy graveyard, which is sparsely populated with headstones huddled together in one corner.

WIXOE

Dedication: St Leonard
No of Bells: 1
Deanery 1836: Clare
Hundred: Risbridge
Union house: Haverhill
Deanery 2000: Clare

3 miles SE of Haverhill between Stoke by Clare & Sturmer. From the A604 take the A1092 nr The Swan for 200 yds then left to Wixoe. O.S. grid ref: TL 718430
Post Code: CO10 8UD

In the 12th c. the Normans constructed this church, as can be seen by the lovely south doorway with its zigzag design around the moulding. The coeval north door is plain. The nave walls are also Norman but have been very much restored over the intervening centuries. The chancel was completely rebuilt and the original apsidal end destroyed during the Victorian era. Above the west end is a wooden weather-boarded bell turret housing one 15th c. bell. There are no signs that a tower ever existed here. Dating from the 14th c. is a very plain octagonal font, not at all like those to which we have become accustomed in Suffolk. In fact the Essex influence is quite strong here, as it is in many of these border parishes. Vladimir Peniakoff (1951), of Popski's Private Army fame, is buried here.

WOOLPIT *****

Dedication:	St Mary
No of Bells:	6
Deanery 1836:	Thedwastre
Hundred:	Thedwastre
Union house:	Onehouse
Deanery 2000:	Lavenham

5 miles NW of Stowmarket on the A14(T). Turn off at the Woolpit turnoff and then bear right, near the recreation ground.
O.S. grid ref: TL 974624
Post Code: IP30 9QG

Someone once described the spire as 'a crown', referring to the flying buttresses, the pinnacles and the parapet. I can see what they meant. The tower and spire were actually rebuilt in the 19th c. It is indeed a beautiful 14th c. church with a magnificent 15th c. entrance porch. Look up at the roof as you enter. Inside the nave you cannot help being impressed by the double hammerbeam roof. The wall-posts have canopied niches and a host of angels look back at you as you marvel at them. A splendid canopy of honour hangs above the chancel arch and the screen. There are more angels in the side aisles. When you tire of looking up, look at the carvings of creatures on the benches. Sitting on a window sill in the north east corner of the nave is the largest wodewose I have ever seen, and the dustiest.

WORDWELL

Dedication: All Saints
No of Bells: 1
Deanery 1836:   Blackbourn
Hundred: Blackbourn
Union house: Bury St Edmunds
Deanery 2000:   Thingoe

3 miles NW of Bury St
Edmunds between Fornham
& Elvedon on the B1106
just south of Wordwell Hall
& next to a pair of cottages.
O.S. grid ref: TL 828720
Post Code: IP28 6UW

Very early signs of building are everywhere, within and without. The quoin stones indicate early Norman, as do the north and south doorways and the tympana above with their unique carvings. Two dogs baying at a tree on one, and a man waving at someone on the other. The church is a treasure. Apart from the west end and bellcote, which is Victorian, and the awful pulpit, what you see is more or less how the Normans built it in the 12th c. What I found fascinating were the carvings on the 15th c. benches (a few are replacements) whimpering dogs, cats doing what cats do, birds, griffins and dragons. On the back of one bench is a scene, probably from a fable, the meaning of which is lost in the mists of time. The church is usually open and is in the hands of The Churches Conservation Trust.

WORLINGTON

Dedication:	All Saints
No of Bells:	5
Deanery 1836:	Fordham
Hundred:	Lackford
Union house:	Mildenhall
Deanery 2000:	Mildenhall

1 mile SW of Mildenhall
on the B1102 Freckenham
road. Turn into Church
Lane at the War Memorial
and follow for 300 yds.
O.S. grid ref: TL 691738
Post Code: IP28 8SG

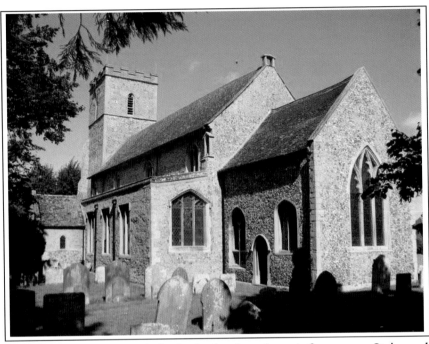

If you find this church locked, the key is not far away. It is well worth having a look round. Both north and south doors are 13th c., as is the chancel, although there are signs of earlier work in the base of the tower. The nave roof is two hammerbeams, alternating with a tiebeam and arch-braced principals. The square font, once plain, is very early but has at some time been re-cut into the form we see today. A tiny part of a wall painting shows on the chancel arch. In the chancel is a dropped-sill sedilia. The piscina, constructed of rescued stone, is in the south aisle. There is a wall monument, of no great age but beautifully carved, to Rice James (1822). The old handcart cum bier is most unusual and was obviously made locally. There is the base of an old churchyard cross in the graveyard east of the chancel.

WORTHAM

Dedication:	St Mary
No of Bells:	1
Deanery 1836:	Hartismere
Hundred:	Hartismere
Union house:	Eye & Wortham
Deanery 2000:	Hartismere

5 miles NW of Eye between Scole & Wattisfield. Turn north off the A143 at the village sign & follow for 1 mile to crossroads.

O.S. grid ref: TM 083788

Post Code: IP22 1SL

The parish sign represents the largest circumference tower in all England, and it is here at Wortham. Twenty-nine feet in diameter with walls over four feet thick. Probably defensive and built before the Normans arrived. Rising above the truncated tower is the wooden bellcote. Inside the Norman nave the roof is single hammerbeam and arch-braced principals, with wall posts set between the twelve windows of the 15th c. clerestory, which illuminates the interior beautifully. The reredos is Victorian and carved from stone. Most charming are the bench carvings, illustrating in words and figures various biblical texts. Unusual too are the Royal Arms of Charles I, which are oval and carved in oak. The altar is made up from the panels of the rood screen. Highly recommended.

WYVERSTONE

Dedication: St George
No of Bells: 3
Deanery 1836: Hartismere
Hundred: Hartismere
Union house: Eye & Worthing
Deanery 2000: Stowmarket

6 miles N of Stowmarket between Finningham & Gt. Ashfield. Turn west off the B1113 at Finningham cross-roads and follow for 1½ m.
O.S. grid ref: TM 042678
Post Code: IP14 4SP

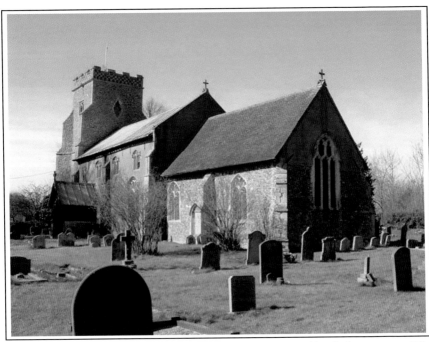

There is a most unusual window in the east wall of the tower. The south porch is a timber construction with a king-post roof, built in the early 15th c. Of the same date is the font with tracery patterns around the bowl. The simple ribbed cover is of the Stuart period. Above, the nave roof is a hammerbeam with arch-braced principals. On one of the principals is a pulley block, once used for raising a rowell to illuminate the rood. I have never seen a pulpit in a worse state. If any sort of professional restoration is required, it is surely here. The beautiful lower parts of the screen, most uncommonly carved in relief, are in a similar condition. Best left like this I suppose, rather than ruined by a coat of varnish. The only thing that looks good in this condition is the mediaeval iron-bound parish chest.

YAXLEY

Dedication:	St Mary
No of Bells:	6
Deanery 1836:	Hartismere
Hundred:	Hartismere
Union house:	Eye & Wortham
Deanery 2000:	Hartismere

1½ mile W of Eye between Eye & Mellis. Turn west off the A140(T) into Yaxley. Church is on the (old) Ipswich Road on a bend. O.S. grid ref: TM 120739 Post Code: IP23 8BX

If you like wood carvings come to Yaxley. The 15th c. lovely stone and flint flushwork on the north porch is more ornate than any other part of the church. It welcomes you into a nave filled with the work of craftsmen. Most unusual perhaps is the 15th c. sexton's wheel. There is only one other in the area, at Long Stratton, Norfolk. There are painted angels around the cornice of the chancel roof and carved bosses at the intersections. Over the chancel arch there is what remains of a doom, and the sawn-off ends of the rood beam remain firmly fixed in the wall. In the eastern bay there are traces of a canopy of honour which once hung here. Below it the screen (until it was reduced) must have been magnificent. The quality of the carving is superb, as is all you see about you, in this lovely church.

235

Ruins and known sites of churches
not mentioned, or locations given, elsewhere.

Parish	Consolidated with ..	OS Map ref.
Brockford	Wetheringsett	?
Chipley in Poslingford	Poslingford	TL 761499
Coclesworth (see p. 61)	Eriswell	TL 723780
Creeting All Saints	Creeting St Mary	TM 093566
Fakenham Parva (see p. 66)	Fakenham Magna	on Euston estate
Flatford	East Bergholt	? (E. Sfk. p. 85)
Haverhill St Botolph	Haverhill St Mary	TL 666454
Horningsheath Parva St Peter	Horringer	TL 823631
Oakley St Andrew	Oakley St Nicholas	TM 147785
Palgrave St John the Baptist	Palgrave	TM 099776
Stowmarket St Mary	Stowmarket	TM 049586
Undley (Domesday reference)	?	nr Lakenheath

There are many other churches in Suffolk mentioned in various sources where the site is uncertain or completely unknown.

Brief notes on lost churches.

The Domesday Book mentions many churches which are unknown to us today. They may have been demolished, they may have been left to rot away as another more substantial church was built nearby. Many of the churches mentioned in Domesday were simple timber constructions, destined to crumble without trace, except perhaps for a post-hole or two.

Occasionally a historical map will show 'Church Field', such as Pannington, near Wherstead. Local historian Zincke believes this indicates a church on the site. It could also be, as at Worlingham Parva, (see E. Sfk. p. 294) where 'St Peter's Meadow' was believed to be the site of Worlingham Parva St Peter's. The true site of the church was discovered 100 yards south of St Peter's Meadow, when a bypass was built in 1977, and the Meadow probably just belonged to the church as glebe land or even a simple reference as to its whereabouts.

Norman Scarfe has compiled a more comprehensive list of churches which were mentioned in Domesday and elsewhere. If your interest is in that direction I commend his books to you.

Amendments to The Parish Churches of East Suffolk.

Shortly after my first book was launched, it was rapidly brought to my attention that I had made some errors and omissions, now corrected below. I would like to apologise unreservedly for these errors and to those affected by them.

CHELMONDISTON St Andrew.

When I wrote about this 'sterilised, hard and stark' church I was unaware that it held a unique place in the history of Suffolk. On December 10th 1944, Chelmondiston church took a direct hit from a German V1 (doodlebug) rocket. Only the tower and part of the chancel were left standing. Therefore much of what is there to be seen today was rebuilt within the same footprint after the war. The church was reconsecrated in 1957. Great store has been set on the unique fact that this was the only church destroyed by enemy action in Suffolk during the war.

Other amendments:

Akenham has been out of regular use since 1972. It is still used for festivals and weddings etc.

Bramford spire is lead, not zinc as I was incorrectly informed.

The 14th c. porch at Bedfield has a crown post, not a king post.

The Henry Moore sculpture *was* the best thing the church at Claydon had to offer. It was removed and is now at Barham.

Ringsfield is 12 miles NW of Southwold, not 2 as stated.

This page has been left deliberately blank, so that it may be removed, and inserted into The Parish Churches of East Suffolk, without causing damage to this volume

Index of names on memorials etc. mentioned in the text.

Chapels of Ease

Chapels of Ease were built for the use of parishioners who lived a distance from the parish church. They never were parish churches as they were generally situated in hamlets or desolate areas away from the populace. Occasionally a disused church was taken back into temporary service while the parish church was being rebuilt. Even then these were never regarded as parish churches, but as chapels of ease instead. Thorpe St Peter's, just 2 miles south of Debenham is an example. It was ruinous in 1602 but rebuilt as a chapel of ease while Ashfield St Mary was being built in 1739 and left to fall back into decay.

Bottesdale's Chapel of Ease is 15th c., built originally as a chantry. Converted into a school in 1561, resurrected as a Chapel of Ease for Redgrave, but has never been afforded the parish church status.

Because this book deals purely with the parish church and usually only the ones with a long history, Chapels of Ease have not been included. Perhaps that is something for the future.

Explanation of Dating System before 1752

Before 1582 the Julian calendar was in use, introduced by Julius Caesar in 43 B.C. Pope Gregory introduced the Gregorian calendar in that year. The year officially began on March 25th (Lady Day) and ended March 24th. All dates between January 1st and March 24th were written thus: 1744/5, for example. 1744 being the March to March year, and 1745 being the January to January year. From March 25th to December 31st the years correspond with each other. In 1751 great changes were introduced and the following year officially began on January 1st 1752. However, there was a discrepancy in the length of the year, and eleven days were omitted from September 1752. September 2nd was followed by September 14th. The days are now automatically adjusted by the introduction of the leap year. In modern terms, a year written as 1744/5 should be regarded as 1745. A year is actually 365.2425 days long.

Churches in Suffolk maintained by
The Churches Conservation Trust

Parish	Dedication	Book*	Page
Akenham	St Mary	E. Sfk.	1
Badley	St Mary	E. Sfk.	11
Bungay	St Mary	E. Sfk.	45
Chilton	St Mary		43
Claydon	St Peter	E. Sfk.	61
Covehithe	St Andrew (ruins)	E. Sfk.	67
Ellough	All Saints	E. Sfk.	87
Icklingham	All Saints		111
Ipswich	St Mary at Quay	E. Sfk.	151
Little Wenham	All Saints	E. Sfk.	176
Newton	All Saints		155
Redgrave	St Mary		170
Rickinghall Superior	St Mary		173
Sapiston	St Andrew		179
South Elmham	All Saints	E. Sfk.	233
Stanton	St John the Baptist (ruin)		188
Stonham Parva	St Mary the Virgin	E. Sfk.	246
Sudbury	St Peter		199
Washbrook	St Mary	E. Sfk.	274
Wordwell	All Saints		231

The Churches Conservation Trust is the national charity that cares for and preserves English churches of historic, architectural or archaeological importance that are no longer needed for regular worship. It promotes public enjoyment of them and their use as an educational and community resource.

If you wish to find out more:

Their website is; www.visitchurches.org.uk

Their address is: 1 West Smithfield, London EC1A 9EE

The book* 'E. Sfk'. referred to above is the companion publication
'A photographic and historic guide to **The Parish Churches of East Suffolk**'

GLOSSARY of Terms, Architectural & Ecclesiastical

Abacus	flat portion on top of a capital.
Aisle	space between an arcade and the outer wall.
Ambulatory	aisle round an apse.
Apse	rounded end (usually of chancel or chapel).
Arcade	row of arches, free-standing and supported on piers or columns; a blind arcade is a dummy.
Arch	can be round-headed; pointed, two-centred or drop, i.e. an arch struck from centre on the springing-line; ogee pointed arch with double curved sides, upper arcs convex, lower concave; lancet pointed arch formed on an acute-angle triangle; and depressed, flattened or elliptical.
Arms	heraldic bearings, heraldic crest.
Ashlar	worked stone with flat surface, usually of regular shape and square edges.
Aumbry	recess to hold sacred vessels, usually with a light or lit candle close by.
Baluster	small (usually circular) supporting columns or posts - as seen on 17th c. communion rails.
Baptistery	a part of the church set aside to accommodate the font.
Barrel roof	like a covered wagon, or inverted ship; barrel vault is a plain vault of uniform cross-section.
Bastion	solid masonry projection.
Batter	inclined face of wall; hence battered and battering.
Battlements	parapet with indentations or embrasures, with raised portions (merlons) between; the gap is called a crenulation.
Bays	internal divisions of building, marked by roof principals or vaulting piers.
Belfry	chamber where the bells are hung in a tower.
Bell chamber	where bells are hung whether or not in a tower.
Bell turret	open stone structure above the roof line containing one or more bells.
Bell cote	small wooden cage like structure containing (usually) one bell.
Billet	log-shape decoration forming part of a moulding.
Benefice	A church office, such as a rectory with fixed capital assets.
Bond	arrangement of bricks or stone in courses.
Box pew	a pew surrounded by a wooden partition with an entrance door for private worship usually for those of higher rank or status than the great unwashed.
Brattice	timber tower, or projecting wooden gallery.
Broach(ed)	having the shape of a spike, with the angle at top more acute than the angle at the bottom.
Buttress	projection from wall etc. for additional support.

BVM   Blessed Virgin Mary.
Canopy of honour   an ornamental roof-like projection above
                (usually) the rood or rood screen. Occasionally over an altar
Capital/cap   the top of a pier or column, upon which the arch rests.
Chamfer   surface made by smoothing off the angle between two stone
                faces.
Chevron   zigzag moulding (Norman, twelfth century).
Cinquefoil   five-lobed.
Clerestory   the part of the nave roof above the side aisles with windows to
                allow more light into the nave
Clunch   hard chalk material.
Cob   unburnt clay mixed with straw.
Coeval   of the same date; contemporary with.
Collar   a timber beam connecting rafters or wall-posts
Corbel   a piece of carved stone or wood which supports a hood-mould
                or part of a roof.
Cornice   decorative projection along top of wall.
Course   level layer of stones or bricks.
Credence shelf   a shelf, usually within the arch of the piscina to hold
                bread or wine, also credence table.
Crenel   gap in battlemented parapet.
Crenellated   embattled or to fortify.
Crocket   carved decoration on the sloping side of a spire or pinnacle
                usually thorn shaped and pointing skyward.
Cupola   a small domed turret on a roof or top of a tower, usually with a
                door.
Cusped /cusping   an upwardly pointed figure created by the intersection
                of two or more arcs or foils.
Decalogue board   a board bearing the Ten Commandments.
Decorated   architectural style around 13th – 14th century. 1280 - 1377.
Diaper work   decoration of squares or lozenges. Trellis-like.
Dogtooth   diagonal indented pyramid or triangle.
Donative   A benefice that can be bestowed by its founder or patron
                without reference to the diocesan authorities ~ adj. consulting
                such a benefice.
Dormer   window placed vertically in sloping roof.
Dressing   carved stonework around openings.
Drystone   un-mortared masonry.
Early English   1175 - 1280.
Embattled   battlemented, with battlements.
Engaged   (column) refers to being attached to the jamb along its length.
                not free-standing. (opp of detached).
English Renaissance Period 1625 - 1700.
Fillet   narrow flat band.

Finial	carving at the apex of an arch, pinnacle spire or roof
Fleche	a slender spire, esp. on a church above an intersection of the nave and transept.
Fleuron	a carved flower.
Flushwork	patterns made in the masonry using flint or stone, neither sunken nor raised.
Fluting	concave mouldings in parallel.
Flying buttress	buttress which is not attached to the wall it supports at the lower portion, to allow passage through, or to save weight, or look more elegant.
Foils	lobes used to embellish the head of an arch or a circular opening. Trefoil. quatrefoil, cinquefoil octofoil etc..
Foliated	carved with leaves.
Footings	bottom part of wall.
Freestone	high-quality sandstone or limestone.
Fresco	painting on wet plaster wall.
Gable	wall covering end of roof-ridge.
Gallery	long passage or room.
Galilee	a small chapel or porch at the west end of some mediaeval churches.
Garderobe	latrine; privy. (wardrobe in Latin)
Gargoyle	a carved stone usually with a spout to throw rainwater well clear of the foundations.
Georgian	period 1700 - 1825.
Gnomon	that part of a sundial which casts the shadow.
Gothic	architectural period 12th - 16th century.
Grisaille	a glass monochrome picture in shades of grey.
Groined	roof with sharp edges at intersection of cross-vaults.
Grotesques	outlandish, distorted or bizarre characterisations of people or animals, not necessarily ugly as in gargoyles.
Half-shaft	roll-moulding on either side of opening.
Hammer-beam	beam jutting out horizontally at right angles at the top of a wall to support other beams and arch-braces
Hanoverian	pertaining to the reign of the House of Hanover, 1714 - 1917
Hatchments	Lozenge shaped frames bearing the coat of arms of a deceased person, made for the funeral and displayed outside the home of the deceased and later retained in the church as a memorial.
Headstock	The wooden beam which carries the weight of a bell.
Heartshrine	a small niche, similar in appearance to a piscina, into which an embalmed heart was placed.
Herringbone	brick or stone laid diagonally.
Hood	arched covering.
Hoodmould	a hood when used to throw off rainwater.

Impost	wall bracket to support arch.
Intramural	within the wall. Early practice of burial for VIPs.
Ionic	order of Greek architecture characterized by a column with scroll-shapes on either side of the capital.
Jacobean	1603 - 1625.
Jamb	side of arch, door or window against which the door/window closes.
Joist	timber stretched from wall-to-wall to support floorboards.
Knop	a decorative knob or boss.
Lancet	(window) long, narrow window with pointed head. (1190 - 1280 in date).
Laudian	Pertaining to Archbishop William Laud (1573 - 1645).
Lintel	horizontal stone or beam bridging opening.
Long and short work	A Saxon technique of having one quoin stone lengthways and the next widthways and so on as the corner progressed upwards.
Loop	narrow opening in a wall
Louvre / louver	(Bell) louver – to allow the sound of bells to escape through the tower wall.
Lucarne	A small slit or opening to allow light into spires and towers.
Mass dial	see Scratch dial.
Mensa	a table usually of stone on stone pillars.
Merlon	solid part of embattled parapet.
Misericord	projection under a choir stall seat serving (when the seat is turned up) to support a person standing, usually carved.
Moulding	masonry decoration.
Mullion	vertical division of window.
Mural	wall or a painting on a wall.
Nailhead	pyramidal moulding.
Needle	A tie beam which passes through a wall, with an eye in the end [like a sewing needle] and through which is passed a cross-member to prevent it withdrawing or the wall/s spreading.
Newel	centre-post of circular staircase.
Niche	a recess usually arched, made in a wall to contain a statue or other object.
Nookshaft	shaft set in angle of jamb or pier.
Norman	1066 – 1190 Romanesque.
Ogee-headed arch	moulding showing in section a double continuous curve, concave below passing into convex above, back to front S.
Oolite	granular limestone.
Open joint	wide, un-mortared space between faces of stones.
Order	relating to the carved sections of an arch or doorway.

Oriel — projecting window in wall; originally a form of porch, often of wood.

Parclose screen — a screen to delineate a private area or to enclose part of the nave for whatever reason.

Parapet — low wall on outer side of main wall.

Parvice — a balcony in front of a church or enclosed courtyard.

Peculiar — a church or parish under the jurisdiction of a diocese different from that in which it lies.

Pediment — low-pitched gable over porticos, doors, windows, etc.

Perpendicular — English architectural style, circa. 1377 - 1547.

Pier — support for arch, usually square as opposed to pillar (round).

Pilaster — shallow pier used to buttress a wall.

Pinnacle — ornament crowning spire, tower etc. or small spire on top of building.

Piscina — basin, usually set in or against wall, with drain for washing vessels after the sacrament.

Pitch — the slope of a roof.

Pitching — rough cobbling.

Plinth — projecting base of wall.

Pointing — mortar or cement in joints between brickwork.

Poppyheads — ornamental carving at the end of church benches and / or pews. *[There are endless variations, very few looking like poppy heads]*

Principal — a main truss or rafter that supports a roof.

Purlin — horizontal timber in a roof supporting rafters.

Quatrefoil — four-lobed.

Quoin — dressed corner stone at the angle of a building.

Refectory — communal dining-hall.

Reliquary — a coffer or shrine for keeping or displaying religious relics.

Reredos — decorative screen behind the altar.

Respond/s — half-piers found in the jambs of arches.

Retable — a frame enclosing carved or painted panels placed at the back of an altar (similar to a reredos).

Reveal — the thickness of the wall from the inside edge, to the window or door.

Rib — raised moulding dividing vault.

Romanesque — prevailing architectural style, eighth to twelfth century, with rounded arches.

Roofridge — summit line of roof.

Rowell — a circular frame with candles placed around the circumference and raised by means of a pulley, to illuminate the rood or canopy of honour.

Glossary (continued)

Royal Arms   the Royal Crest authorised by the Monarch of the day. These vary in size and are usually painted locally.

Rubble   un-squared stone/s not laid in courses.

Rustication   worked ashlar stone, with faces left deliberately rough.

Sacristy   a room in a church to house the sacred vessels and vestments, similar in use to a vestry, and sometimes used as such.

Saltire   a diagonal; equal-limbed diagonal cross. St Andrew's style cross.

Sanctuary   the part of a church nearest to the altar, usually behind the altar rail.

Saxon   pre 1066.

Scratch dial   a crude sundial with central hole (into which is inserted a gnomon) with rays usually scratched on a buttress or quoin-stone of a church to show the time of the next service, also mass-dial.

Sciapus   legendary Scandinavian figure with enormous feet.

Sedilia *[pl.]*   seats for clergy during parts of long mediaeval masses (usually in or on the south wall of the sanctuary, often a dropped window sill.) *[singular: 'sedile']*

Septaria   A semi-hard brownish clay-like stone with calcite bonding.

Serpent   18th c. deep-toned wind instrument,

Seven Sacraments (The)   Baptism, Holy Communion, Confirmation, Holy Orders, Reconciliation, Matrimony & Anointing of the sick.

Shaft   narrow column. i.e. supporting the font.

Shingle   a wooden tile, usually of cedar.

Soffit   underside of arch, opening or eaves.

Sounding board   see Tester.

Spandrel   the space (roughly triangular in shape each side) between an arch and it's square hood-mould. Also found in roofs in the space between the beam and arch-brace and/or rafter

Splay   chamfer, or sloping face. Window reveal, wider on the inner wall than at the window.

Squint   observation hole in wall or room.

Stoup   a carved bowl for holding holy water to purify oneself before, or as, entering the church.

Stringcourse   continuous horizontal mouldings on a wall-face.

Stuart   pert. to the reign of House of Stuart, 1603 - 1707.

Sundial   to indicate the time (of the next service), usually on the south porch gable or on the tower.

Tester   a suspended canopy over a pulpit also 'a sounding board'.

Tie beam   large horizontal beam at the base of a roof (or top of a wall) to
            prevent the walls spreading outwards with the weight of the
            roof. Occasionally piercing the wall and pinned-through
            outside. (see Needle)

Tracery   intersecting rib-work in upper part of window or decoratively
            carved in wood.

Transept   either or both of the arms of a cross-shaped church at right
            angles to the main body of the church. Usually North or South.

Transom   horizontal division of window.

Trefoil   three-lobed.

Tudor   Elizabethan, 1547 - 1600.

Turret   small tower, round or polygonal, tapered or straight.

Tympanic   pertaining to the tympanum.

Tympanum   the stonework filling the space between the horizontal lintel of a
            doorway and the arch above it. *pl.* tympana.

Victorian   pert. to the reign of Queen Victoria, 1837 - 1901.

Volute   decorative spiral scroll in stonework found on some Ionic
            capitals.

Voussoir   wedge-shaped stone forming part of an arch, not the keystone.

Wag(g)on roof   see Barrel roof.

Wainscote   a panel on the lower portion of a wall, in a different material
            from that of the upper part, usually wood.

Wainscotting   plural of wainscote.

Wall-stair staircase built into thickness of wall. as rood-stairs.

Weathering sloping surface to throw off rainwater on buttresses and
            battlements etc..

Wodewose or Woodwose. Wild man with beard carrying a club. Usually found
            on the base of a font accompanied by lions. *(occasionally
            erroneously referred to as a Woodhouse)*

Basic Roof styles

Arch braced with possible (vertically variable) position of collar

Arch-braced single hammerbeam

Arch-braced double hammerbeam

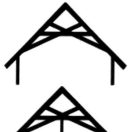

Scissor beams

Scissor beams with tie beam and king post [one post]

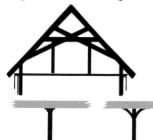

Scissor beams with tie beam and queen posts [two posts]

left.   King-post
right. Crown- post [crown-post has quadrilateral supports]

253

Notes

Notes

Notes

Notes

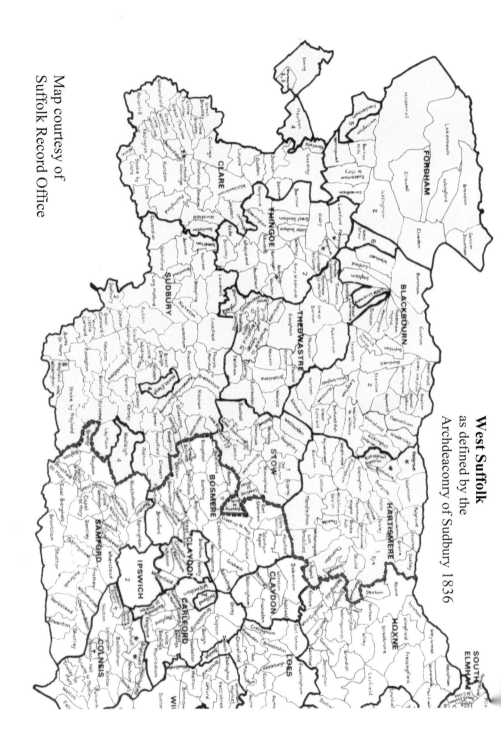

Map courtesy of
Suffolk Record Office

West Suffolk
as defined by the
Archdeaconry of Sudbury 1836